# INSIDE *the* WORLD *of* BRIDGERTON

*For Mr C and Pippa, for keeping the teapot filled*

# INSIDE *the* WORLD *of* BRIDGERTON

## TRUE STORIES OF REGENCY HIGH SOCIETY

### CATHERINE CURZON

UNOFFICIAL

Michael O'Mara Books Limited

First published in Great Britain in 2023 by
Michael O'Mara Books Limited
9 Lion Yard
Tremadoc Road
London SW4 7NQ

A CIP catalogue record for this book is available from the British Library.

This product is made of material from well-managed, FSC®-certified forests
and other controlled sources. The manufacturing processes conform to the
environmental regulations of the country of origin.

ISBN: 978-1-78929-499-6 in hardback print format
ISBN: 978-1-78929-500-9 in ebook format

1 2 3 4 5 6 7 8 9 10

Main cover image: Lee Avison / Trevillion Images
Cover graphics: digiselector / depositphotos.com
Cover design © The Brewster Project
Designed and typeset by Claire Cater

Printed and bound by CPI Group (UK) Ltd, Croydon, CR0 4YY

www.mombooks.com

MIX
Paper | Supporting
responsible forestry
FSC
www.fsc.org
FSC® C171272

# CONTENTS

# A REGENCY TIMELINE

'If George IV ever had a friend – a devoted friend – in any rank of life, we protest that the name of him or her has not yet reached us. An inveterate voluptuary, especially if he be an artificial person, is of all known beings the most selfish. Selfishness is the true repellent of human sympathy. Selfishness feels no attachment, and invites none; it is the charnel house of the affections.'

Funeral of George IV

1738    George III is born.

1760    With the death of George II, the reign of George III begins.

1761    George III and Charlotte of Mecklenburg-Strelitz are married.

1762    George IV (initially Prince of Wales, later the Prince Regent) is born.

1785    George IV and Maria Fitzherbert are illegally and secretly married.

1788    George III's first serious mental illness prompts the Regency Crisis. Happily, sanity and order are restored.

1795    George IV and Caroline of Brunswick are married.

1796    Princess Charlotte of Wales, the only child of George IV and Caroline of Brunswick, is born.

1803    The Napoleonic Wars begin.

1804    Napoleon is proclaimed Emperor of the French.

1805    Admiral Lord Nelson is killed during the triumphant Battle of Trafalgar.

1806    William Pitt the Younger, the youngest Prime Minister ever to hold office, dies.

1807    An Act for the Abolition of the Slave Trade, the culmination of decades of work, is passed in the House of Commons. The following year, the slave trade is formally abolished in the British colonies.

1810    George III is declared insane after years of health struggles; he can no longer reign as King.

1811    The Prince of Wales is made Prince Regent and the Regency begins. *Bridgerton* fans everywhere rejoice!

1812    Prime Minister Spencer Perceval is assassinated. To date, he remains the only British Prime Minister to die in this way.

1814    The First Bourbon Restoration returns the French monarch to the throne.

1815    Napoleon returns to France and the Hundred Days begins. His defeat by Wellington at Waterloo marks the end of the Napoleonic Wars.

1815    The Second Bourbon Restoration returns the French monarch to the throne. Again.

1816    The Year Without a Summer strikes the United Kingdom. Those flimsy frocks suddenly looked flimsier than ever.

1817    The first cholera pandemic begins.

1817 Princess Charlotte of Wales, the only child of the Prince Regent (later George IV) and heir to the throne, dies. She leaves no heir, so Prinny's brothers begin a panicked search for wives of their own to secure the line of succession.

1818 Charlotte of Mecklenburg-Strelitz dies. Pannier and wigmakers everywhere watch their court business die with her.

1819 The Peterloo Massacre shocks the nation and makes Prinny more unpopular than ever.

1820 George III dies in seclusion at Windsor. The Prince Regent is crowned King George IV.

1820 The enormously popular Queen Caroline is put on trial under the Pains and Penalties Bill in an effort to secure a divorce for George IV. The effort fails.

1821 Napoleon dies.

1830 George IV dies in seclusion at Windsor, ravaged by alcohol, laudanum and years of hard living. *The Times* skewered him with a savage, unflinching obituary.

King George III, widely known in history as 'mad King George', had a turbulent time on the throne, experiencing myriad health issues, leading eventually to the Regency, and overseeing the loss of the American colonies.

# INTRODUCTION

**'Dearest Gentle Reader ... did you miss me?'**

Lady Whistledown, *Bridgerton*

hen Lady Whistledown speaks, the glittering, glamourous, gorgeous denizens of *Bridgerton*'s Regency world listen. Whether between the covers of a book or in the enormously successful Netflix adaptation, Julia Quinn's smash-hit stories have captured imaginations across the globe. The comings and goings of the *haut ton* are as irresistible today as ever, and in a rustle of silk and a tangle of bedsheets they've shown devoted Bridgertonians that life in the Regency wasn't all assembly rooms and handsome dukes – though they certainly had their part to play. From cradle to grave, via the marriage mart, killer cosmetics and everything in between, navigating the world of *le bon ton* could be as complicated as the most complex Regency dance. The rewards for those who conquered the *beau monde* were immense, yet in a time when status and class were everything, there were plenty of places where even the daintiest deb could stumble.

The mysterious Lady Whistledown knows the world of *Bridgerton* better than anybody. If there's gossip, she hears it; if there's drama, she shares it, and all with a sweep of her very genteel pen. In Regency Britain, after all, appearances were everything. We might dismiss the effortlessly polite Lady Whistledown as a work of fiction, but she certainly had her counterparts in reality. Gossip-hungry readers of *Town and Country Magazine* flicked straight to the 'Tête-à-Tête' section to read redacted reports of who was doing what to whom, and coffee houses buzzed with discussion of the latest drama among the rich and famous. Meanwhile, wide-eyed daughters were thrust into the spotlight of the marriage market in their search for the most eligible bachelors, and an invitation to the court of the salacious Regent was the true sign that one had made an impact in the ongoing battle to conquer the ton.

At the very top of the tree sat the Prince Regent, resplendent in the opulent rooms of Carlton House or beneath the rococo domes of John Nash's eye-popping seaside wonder, the Royal Pavilion. The Regent, aka *Prinny*, was a man who positively courted scandal even as he presided over the pinnacle of fashion, luxury and high living. His official marriage to his cousin Caroline of Brunswick had collapsed in spectacularly public style, and his secret marriage to commoner Maria Fitzherbert had been on and off again more times than his breeches, but as the gentleman at the heart of the Regency, this spendthrift ladies' man reigned over all he could see.

The Prince Regent, later King George IV, was a dandy and *bon vivant*, well known for his frivolous lifestyle and famous to all *Bridgerton* fans as the man at the top of *le bon ton*.

The Prince Regent, later King George IV, had come to power thanks to the indisposition of his father, George III.

The unfortunate sovereign and his wife, Queen Charlotte of Mecklenburg-Strelitz, were married in 1761, just a year after the then twenty-two-year-old George III assumed the throne. The Prince Regent was the oldest of their fifteen children and a man who was a constant thorn in the side of his pious, reserved parents. They opposed virtually everything he stood for, from politics to his chaotic personal life, but as the years passed and the monarch succumbed to mental illness, it became obvious to everyone that the then Prince of Wales would be in power sooner rather than later.

By 1811, King George III was, in the language of the time, mad. His mental problems were accompanied by a host of physical challenges, from blindness to immobility, and he could no longer hope to reign. Under the guidance of his devoted wife and carer Charlotte, and the Tory government that he had always supported against the wishes of his son, George III had no choice but to surrender power. George, Prince of Wales, became the Prince Regent, and Britain would never be quite the same again.

The court of George III and Queen Charlotte had been a place of intense formality and tradition. *Bridgerton* viewers will be familiar with the Queen's elaborate wardrobe, filled with ornate powdered wigs and enormous panniers that appear out of date and old-fashioned against the Empire-line dresses and simple hairstyles of the younger ladies. This juxtaposition perfectly illustrates the different worlds in which Charlotte and her eldest son moved. She was a product of another age, an age that was dying with the old King, and the Prince Regent and the ton were moving along without her.

The Regent reigned for almost ten years before he became King George IV on the death of his father. During that decade it seemed as though a new world was born. Modern aesthetics swept through fashion and architecture, and the worlds of industry, military and business expanded at a breathless rate. In the first twenty years of the nineteenth century, victories at Trafalgar and Waterloo kept Britain at the forefront of contemporary superpowers, while at home industrial growth was driving innovation forwards and making the rich richer still, even as workers rioted and the poorest went hungry.

It is against this backdrop that Lady Whistledown watches the intrigues of the Bridgerton family and those who feud with them, love them and offer them a listening ear. From health to wealth and romance to royalty, this book is your guide to the world of the ton in which the Bridgertons and their circle moved.

CHAPTER ONE

# CLASS AND THE TON

**'Although there are among the highest ranks of society in the United Kingdom many excellent characters, who do honour to the exalted stations they fill in the State … yet it is to be lamented, that there are not a few who pursue an opposite course … their time is chiefly spent either at the gaming table, or in pursuit of the most frivolous and contemptible amusements, sinking in the view of society that respectability and consequence in the state, which their birth and fortune had assigned them.'**

Patrick Colquhoun, *A Treatise on the Wealth, Power, and Resources of the British Empire, in Every Country of the World*[1]

s Lady Whistledown and those in her column knew, nothing kept the social wheels of Regency Britain turning like the rigidly observed class system. The class into which a person was born could make or break them and determine the path of their whole life. It would dictate their educational opportunities, their career prospects and every part of their existence from cradle to grave. It certainly determined how one was looked upon by others. Moving between the social classes was a delicate business indeed, and one that few were able to pull off.

Bridgertonians have all heard of the ton, the social set in which their heroes and heroines exist. The ton was the highest of high society in the Regency era, and for those who weren't born into that rank, infiltrating it was far easier said than done. It wasn't impossible, but nor was it something that could happen overnight; in some cases it took literally generations. The ton was unforgiving in its strict enforcement of hierarchy, and its members came from royalty, aristocracy and the gentry. Money, ancestry and even manners played their part, and to break the established, unspoken rules of the ton could spell social death.

The ton presided over Regency society like a military dictatorship. Very few could be said to be the arbiters of the system, but power was wielded by everyone from the Regent himself to tastemaker Beau Brummell, to the famed and feared Lady Patronesses of Almack's, London's most elite assembly rooms. Their word could make or break a reputation, and it was they who decided who did and didn't receive coveted invitations to their sought-after events. These were usually held during the Season, which occurred between late January and early July, namely the time when Parliament was sitting. During these months, the capital was the social heart of the ton, where families would try to pair off their unmarried children in the unforgiving marriage mart.

A mistake made here could stick for life, and one had to be sure to follow the finely honed, sometimes bewildering class rules if one were to stand a chance of becoming a leader of the ton. For a girl to miss out on a proposal in her first Season wasn't quite the end of the world, but it was close. With each subsequent year her chances became less and less promising and the pool that was open to her of 'leading personages in High Life who are enjoying the festivities of the season in London' less and less impressive.[2] To risk being left on the shelf is something we'll come to later.

# KEEPING IT CLASSY

Class in the Regency era wasn't a complicated business as such, but it was far more intricate than we might expect. Rather than the three obvious categories of upper, middle and working class, things were a lot more nuanced for those who lived under the reign of the Regent. Thankfully, in 1814 Patrick Colquhoun provided a breakdown of the classes and who fitted into which in his book *A Treatise on the Wealth*,

*Power, and Resources of the British Empire.* Like so many other things in those tumultuous years, outlining the social classes wasn't as simple as it might at first seem.

Colquhoun divided the classes into eight, beginning with Highest Orders and ending with a special reserved category for the army and the navy. In between those two divisions, he assigned each and every member of British society to one class or another. At the top, in the Highest Orders, were royalty and aristocrats, the most senior churchmen and officers of state and all families above the rank of baronet.

During the Regency era, one thing was instrumental in deciding a person's class: birthright. At the top of the heap sat the royal family, the latest in the line that had come over from Hanover with George I in 1714. The history of the Hanoverian monarchs was rich with feuding and scandal, but George III and Charlotte of Mecklenburg-Strelitz had tried to arrest the rot. They lived lives that would be familiar to any upper-middle-class family of the era, eschewing the political wheeling and dealing that had characterized the reign of George II and the opulent decadence that would later define that of the Prince Regent. The King was known to his subjects by the affectionate nickname 'Farmer George', thanks to his love of working the land, and he believed that hard work on earth would find its reward in heaven. Rejecting opulence and needless shows of wealth and privilege – the Queen's jewellery chest excepted – George III and Charlotte tried, and in most cases failed, to instil this same sense of humility, hard work and religious piety into their children.

The King suffered several periods of ill health, each worse than that which preceded it. The Regency had almost come into being decades earlier when he suffered a mental collapse, but at the last minute George III's wits were restored and he was able to take control once more. Yet as the years passed his relapses became more regular and more severe. Under the treatment of the fearsome Dr Francis Willis and his physician sons, King George III was subjected to brutal and humiliating medical treatments. He was restrained, his head shaved and his body covered in leeches. Blisters were drawn on his neck, his mouth was stuffed with rags to keep him silent, and he was isolated from his wife and children, who grew terrified of the man who had once been a loving spouse and father. Eventually the King's wits collapsed completely, and Farmer George was left a shadow of the man he had once been, whispered about as 'the mad King'. Something had to be done.

By the time of the Regency, three of the royal couple's fifteen children had died. Of those who remained, the boys had all stirred up some scandals of their own, while the girls had never had the chance. Only one daughter, Charlotte, the Princess Royal, had been permitted to marry before the King became unwell. The remaining daughters were kept sheltered by their mother, who drew them to her in an insular and unhappy world, insisting on their companionship as her beloved husband sank further and further into madness. In the tightly controlled Regency marriage mart, the princesses had no chance of escape once Queen Charlotte had pulled up the drawbridge. For those who eventually managed to find a husband and make their escape, it took decades.

The reign of George III had been enormously tumultuous. It was riven by political intrigue and infighting, and the King's health had suffered a shattering blow from the American War of Independence, which resulted in the loss of the North American colonies. The royal palaces rang with conflict too, as the Prince of Wales, later to reign as Prince Regent, ran up eye-watering debts, cast off mistresses at a rate of knots and generally served as a sharp thorn in his parents' side. By the time the Regency finally came into being his worst excesses were behind him and he was his mother's strongest rock, but scandal and gossip still followed in his wake wherever he went. It didn't help that his ongoing efforts to divorce his fun-loving wife, Caroline of Brunswick, were continually frustrated by her public popularity.

The Prince of Wales had married his cousin, Caroline of Brunswick, in 1795. By agreeing to the marriage he secured the payment of his debts, but the couple were miserable from the start. At their first meeting, George called for brandy and his mother's sympathetic ear, while Caroline asked where the handsome prince she had been anticipating might be found. The prince was drunk at the wedding ceremony and passed out on the floor of the bedchamber that night, yet somehow they did manage to produce an heir. The couple separated soon after the birth of their only child, Princess Charlotte, and as George's popularity plummeted, Caroline's soared. For the next two decades she was celebrated as a public favourite and one of the few people who refused to be cowed by the Prince of Wales. Even as King, he was never able to achieve the one thing he wanted: a divorce.

The Prince of Wales and Caroline of Brunswick had a relationship envied by none. Immediately put off by his wife's pungent stench and plain looks, George tried and failed to dissolve the marriage as soon as he became King, proving that even the most powerful in society were beholden to its rules.

The Regent himself was immensely unpopular with the people of Great Britain, who stoned his carriage and greeted him in the streets with 'vociferations personally offensive to the Prince Regent'.[3] But as the nation's coffers were exhausted by war and poverty and starvation hit the poorest hard, the Regent went on spending. He filled his opulent homes with priceless antiques and appeared at the most expensive places with a glittering array of fashionable friends and mistresses with 'nothing but a hand to accept pearls and diamonds with, and an enormous balcony to wear them on'.[4]

As the people starved and the Queen grew gaunt and grey with the strain of caring for her husband, Prinny draped his conquests in jewels, packed his palaces with gold and gadded about as though he was already the King. The people of France had already lopped the head off their own monarch and sent his heirs into exile or to unmarked graves, and when protestors daubed 'Bread or the Regent's Head' on the walls of Carlton House, the country stood on the very brink of revolution. Thankfully, cool political heads were able to see off the threat, but the Prince Regent's tastes are stamped all over what we recognize today as the Regency style.

Immediately beneath royalty came the nobility, or some of them. Those who held hereditary titles, though not honorary titles, were the crème de la crème of the ton. These denizens of the House of Lords lived off their assets, and their families were on first-name terms with their fellow patrons at White's and Brooks's, while their wives and daughters clutched their vouchers for Almack's in excited hands. Any Bridgertonian will be familiar with their fair share of dukes, but the class was also occupied by marquises, earls, viscounts, barons and their families. Each title brought with it a new step on the order of rank, and each step made a family that little bit more desirable, whether in business, marriage or simply social life. To hobnob with a duke and duchess would always trump a visit from a baron and baroness – but nothing could top an invitation from royalty itself.

In the second class came the gentry. These were gentlemen with the rank of baronet or below, knights, country gents and those who lived on the largest incomes but held no hereditary title. To be considered a member of the landed gentry, one must own in excess of 300 acres of land – unthinkable for the vast majority of the country, who were more likely to be tenants than landlords. Landowners also enjoyed the right to vote, which ensured that Parliament was controlled by this class until 1832, when reform swept the system under the reign of William IV. Though the members of this class might reap the trappings of wealth, from sprawling estates to a bustling domestic staff and the best of everything, such as imported silks and bespoke coaches pulled by the finest horses, those who held titles in this sect didn't sit in the House of Lords. That alone rendered them just a little less desirable in the pecking order of the ton.

As you might expect, the third class and those beneath it were considerably less illustrious. There were no titles to be found, and in the cases of those at the lower end of the scale, not very much of anything. There was certainly no possibility of existing in the world of the ton unless something were to change significantly.

The fourth class was that of professionals, such as teachers, doctors and merchants. There was also special dispensation for respectable shopkeepers, artists and similar, essentially anyone who took a modest income. Such an income was required for the fifth class too, where innkeepers and the like rubbed shoulders, far below the ton. Beneath them sat the sixth class, where labourers, artisans and those deemed menial were to be found. Few would want to fall into the seventh class, which Colquhoun peopled with paupers, rogues, criminals and everyone who was left. The list ended with a special category reserved for members of the army and the navy, who were exempted – for now – from inclusion in the other, ranked classes.

# THE REGENCY GENT

'*Mauvaise honte* is that awkward bashfulness we perceive in young people when they appear in the presence of those whom they conceive to be in a

**more exalted sphere of life than themselves … Every young gentleman, when arrived at manhood; if he be a gentleman by birth, by fortune, by profession or education; if he have done nothing to degrade himself, is fit company for a prince, and this *mauvaise honte* arises from his not having a consciousness of it.'**

John Trusler, *A System of Etiquette*[5]

The concept of being a gentleman was very important to those who lived in the Regency period, but it wasn't some nebulous thing. Today we are used to saying someone is behaving like a gentleman when they are considerate or polite, but in the long eighteenth century a badly behaved man could still be a gentleman, so long as he had the social standing to guarantee the title. During the Regency, a gentleman was essentially a man who came from the upper classes, including peers, baronets, knights and squires, and he was usually – but not always – born into the position.

The first assumption we might make is that all gentlemen owned land and property, but it was a little more nuanced than that. Really, the key qualification was that a gentleman didn't work for a living; instead, he made money from rent paid by tenants if he was a landowner, as well as good investments, annuities and similar. It wasn't enough to be born into a titled family either, because simply having a title didn't give one a seat in the Lords. That distinction was a particularly important one, and one that's easy to trip over today, though it certainly wasn't during the Regency. Crucially, our gentleman would never have to get his hands dirty in return for a wage packet.

If a man was born the eldest son of a gentleman and stood to inherit wealth and land, especially an estate, then he was a gentleman from the off. The minimum territory even to be within a whisper of being considered a gentleman was 300 acres, but the more he could claim as his own, the more elevated and enviable his status.

Of course, in a world of heirs and spares, there can only be one oldest son and heir, leaving those sons that followed after with a slightly trickier proposition. On the face of it they would never inherit, but as the sons and brothers of gentlemen they were deserving of the title even though they had to earn their living. So, in a world where no gentleman would ever be put in the awkward position of being paid to do a job, what was he to do? The answer was having an honorarium. The gentlemanly professions were limited but included careers such as having an office in the clergy, becoming an officer in the military or practising as a barrister or physician. Because all these respectable positions required an investment upfront, whether to train or to buy a commission, they carried with them a level of exclusivity which only those with money could attain. Once a role had been secured, our young gentlemen weren't paid a wage but given an honorarium, which was a payment offered in recognition of them lending their time, rather than a salary. It was an important distinction, for no gentleman would ever be paid for his labour; an honorarium was a gesture of gratitude, rather than an exchange of money for services.

Being a 'gentleman' in the Regency was less about behaviour and more about social standing. As long as a man had wealth and position he was deemed worthy of the title, no matter what his conduct suggested.

Of all these professions, a military officer was the highest status for a man to land. He achieved this by buying a commission to the rank of officer, an opportunity reserved only for men who could afford it, with many choosing to believe that this was also a guarantee of good character. It wasn't, of course. Men who purchased a commission were also assured that the payment they made would be held in trust until they left the service, when they would receive the money back to see them through their retirement. The honorarium they secured during the years they spent in the forces would be equivalent to an interest payment on the investment, which certainly wasn't enough to live the high life. For this reason, the families of officers often gave their sons allowances so they could top up their honorarium and live in the manner to which a gentleman was accustomed. Jane Austen's Captain Wentworth made out rather better; he went away a hopeful naval officer and came back a captain with £30,000 to his name, equivalent to nearly £3 million today. Not a bad payday by any standards!

Anyone who knows their way around Regency literature will be familiar with the concept of a younger brother going into the clergy. In this profession, the holder was given something known as 'a living', which provided the clergyman with money and a place to live. To enter the clergy, a gentleman had to first secure both an Oxbridge degree and a testimonial from his college that recommended him to serve the Church. The testimonial would be approved by a bishop, and the candidate would then undertake an examination that would establish both his fluency in Latin and his knowledge and understanding of scripture. If he successfully passed the exam, he was all set to embark on a career initially as a deacon, after which he was finally ordained. Only then could he obtain a living of his own, a process that could take anything from a week to a decade.

Without this, it was impossible for anyone to become a vicar. Though we may still talk of 'earning a living' today, in the Regency it meant having a parish church of one's own, complete with a parsonage and perhaps even lands that could be rented out. Here, the gentleman vicar would carry out his duties in return for a financial consideration funded by tithes. Of course, the easiest and quickest way to find a good living was to have one in the family. An advowson was a patronage that gave the person who held it the right to appoint the cleric of their choice to a vacant living, and an advowson could be bought and sold just like a piece of property. With advowsons costing several times the value of the living, holding one was for the wealthy only. If a hopeful vicar had a family member with the right of advowson who was happy to give him a living, he was home and dry. Barring the unlikely event of the bishop taking a dislike to a clergyman and removing him from his position, it was a job and a house for life. Even better, the enterprising vicar could eventually seek permission from his bishop to slough off the actual work he was expected to do to a young curate who was looking to one day get a living of his own.

Life as a vicar was not, however, one of unbridled wealth. They received the lesser tithes of the parish – 10 per cent of its produce and livestock – which could be anything from a meagre purse to a considerable income. Of course, they also received a home and just like their officer brothers could sometimes turn to a family allowance to top up their lifestyle. Regardless, a vicar was a gentleman, and that was all that mattered.

For those who chose the law, one thing was paramount: to be considered a gentleman, one must pursue a career not as a solicitor but as a barrister. While the middle-class solicitor was certainly respectable, only a barrister could call himself a gentleman, and to achieve the role meant a high financial outlay. Barristers began their careers at university – preferably a prestigious institution – then applied for a position at the Inns of Court, essentially a law school of sorts. Once their period at the Inns of Court was over, the barristers who had been observing them selected the candidates who would be called to the Bar, which meant they would become trial lawyers. Unsuccessful candidates were instead destined to become solicitors, so near and yet so far from establishing themselves as gentlemen.

Unlike solicitors, who were paid for their services, barristers received money by way of a gratuity from their clients. From this money, they would pay solicitors a fee for bringing them cases. Becoming a barrister was a sure way to be recognized as a gentleman, and it was also an excellent way to make it into senior government appointments or even Cabinet positions. The gratuities were high and the social circles impressive; for any gent, it was an excellent position to obtain, though not an easy one to secure.

If the military, the clergy and the law didn't appeal, there was one last avenue open to the would-be gentleman: medicine. Just as the solicitor and barrister occupied different rungs on the social ladder, so too were there important distinctions when it came to the world of medicine. No gentleman would ever be a surgeon; if one wanted to be respectable, one had to establish oneself as a physician. Just as the barrister and clergyman had to attend university before they could enter their profession, in order to differentiate themselves from the untrained doctors and surgeons who proliferated throughout the Georgian era, the Regency gentleman who wanted to make his living in this field had first to secure a place at a reputable medical school. In that way, he could be sure to obtain an official medical licence, which was certainly the badge of a more genteel sort of medic.

Once a physician had secured his licence, he was free to begin practice and start building what he no doubt hoped would be a wealthy and illustrious list of clients. Once again, he wouldn't receive a salary but instead would be paid a gratuity by his patients. Though these gratuities would guarantee a modest living for a gentleman, honing one's expertise as well as one's register of patrons was the gateway to a far more rewarding life. After all, if a physician could land himself a rich family who kept him on permanent retainer and recommended him to their equally monied friends, the sky was the limit.

*There is no being a real gentleman, without honor,*
*and a becoming pride; and surely there is no becoming*
*pride in seduction, for the seducer in any shape is a*
*rascal, and lost to every sense of virtue, and of honor.*[6]

Yet if being a gentleman was less about behaviour than about how one made money, it introduced an interesting dichotomy. A man who behaved like a gentleman might never officially become one, while a 'gentleman' who lived off his assets and lands could behave as anything but and never lose the honour of the title society bestowed on him. It was one of the many contradictions of the ton.

# A REGENCY LADY

'Let religion and morality be the foundation of the female character … We may safely teach a well-educated girl that virtue ought to wear an inviting aspect; that it is due to her excellence to decorate herself with comely apparel – but we must never cease to remember that it is VIRTUE we seek to adorn.'

Anonymous, *The Mirror of the Graces*[7]

So far, we've spent a fair amount of time thinking about gentlemen, but the Regency woman is equally deserving of a detailed examination. Owning land or establishing a respectable profession simply didn't come into it. Instead, to be considered a lady required a completely different set of skills, and these were judged in a completely different manner. While even the worst-behaved gentleman was still a gentleman, the status of lady – if not the officially bestowed title – could be snatched away with one wrong move.

The Regency woman was expected to have one ambition, and that was to become a lady. Not necessarily to hold the title of Lady, but to be spoken of as one by those who knew her. As far as received wisdom went, that was the highest honour she could hope to attain. To this end, her education was not one that would end in university and a career; it was tailored towards a very different destiny. As we'll see when we tackle the bewildering world of the marriage mart and courtship in Regency times, the options for young ladies were limited once they had come out – of that, more later – and marriage was goal number one, whether they liked it or not.

Though a young lady might well have ambitions beyond marriage, it wasn't considered proper for her to voice them, let alone pursue them. She needn't trouble her pretty head with ideas of a career or any of that nonsense, because that wasn't her destiny. Instead, she was expected to catch the eye of the most eligible bachelor she could, then work on hooking him, reeling him in and getting herself married off. Then she could set about producing her heir and her spare and becoming the next generation's Lady Danbury. Yet whether she was as kind-hearted as Daphne Bridgerton or as scheming as Cressida Cowper, the Regency young lady would have been through an education that was as regimented in its way as anything her brothers might face. For the likes of Eloise Bridgerton, who felt the restrictions of femininity and society's expectations so keenly, it must have been stifling.

> *It is in vain to expend large sums of money and large portions of time in the acquirement of accomplishments, unless some attention be also paid to the attainment of a certain grace in their exercise, which, though a circumstance distinct from themselves, is the secret of their charm and pleasure-exciting quality.*[8]

If a young lady was to show off her accomplishments, she was limited to demonstrating the qualities that would make her a good wife and, in the future, a good mother. She was destined to become a society hostess who should never attempt to challenge her spouse intellectually, even if she was in reality more than capable of doing so. Beauty was one thing, but looks didn't guarantee that a lady would be able to manage a household nor make a good impression with her husband's influential friends. She needed a respectable family, a decent dowry and some very specific qualities that had been drilled into her since childhood. These accomplishments were intended to show her off to her very best, and of course the more accomplishments she could master the better the indication that her family were well able to afford the tutors, dance masters and other experts needed to shape their pupil.

In order to secure a worthy husband, Regency ladies had to master a number of skills, including but not limited to fluency in languages, the art of beautiful lettering and a talent for music. And what better way to show off family wealth than to pay for the best tutors available to teach an accomplished young woman?

It's important to note that there were obvious exceptions to all these rules, but they were few and far between – no doubt to the chagrin of some young ladies whose interests extended beyond those that were commonly accepted. In the upper classes, mothers oversaw the education of their daughters at home, and it wasn't usual for a girl to be sent off to school. Anne 'Gentleman Jack' Lister, of course, is one of the more famous names who did go to boarding school, but her situation was not the experience of most genteel young ladies.

Everything was a symbol of prestige if you just knew how to show it off, and the accomplishments of debutantes – about whom we'll learn more later – were no different, whether scholarly or artistic. The first and most basic ability a lady must master was that of reading. Though this may seem pretty obvious, reading was how she would both pick up bon mots and learn intelligent conversation, though God forbid she form strong opinions. An interest in the rights of women, such as that Eloise developed, was certainly not encouraged. An ability to read would also mean that, in adulthood, our young lady would be able to answer her correspondence each morning and ensure that her household was properly run. Of course, *what* she read was another matter, and the books she was given were subject to some very careful selection by parents and governesses. Some sciences were acceptable, such as Queen Charlotte's favourite pastime of botany, but the likes of anything beyond basic politics and philosophy were definitely off-limits. George III even rejected a possible marriage match because the princess in question had an interest in philosophy and he suspected that it augured ill for the future. Young ladies were allowed to read anything that might improve them or make them pleasant companions, and they were expected to be able to read aloud for the entertainment of their family and guests too. If a girl couldn't master that, she had a long road ahead of her, because sparkling conversation was the cornerstone of virtually every social engagement she would face.

Of course, not everything a lady read was for the good of her social accomplishments. Who could resist a dip into the fashion magazines that even the likes of Queen Charlotte and her daughters read, which were full of society news and who was wearing what, as well as where they were spotted and with whom. Without Lady Whistledown's pamphlet to let our ladies know what was going on sartorially and socially, where would the families of *Bridgerton* be?

The natural companion to reading is, of course, writing, and our Regency young ladies approached their studies of writing in two ways. Firstly, being a respectable member of the ton entailed a regular back and forth of correspondence, and when a lady settled at her bureau in her morning dress each day, correspondence was the only thing on her mind. It was how she kept in touch with what was happening among her family and circle and, crucially, how she kept the social wheel turning. She had to keep up to date, or how on earth would she know the ins and outs of all the gossip from Almack's?

Today, when we dash off a text or email with barely a second thought, it can be mystifying to realize how different it was for ladies in the Regency. That's where the second element of their writing studies came in: the art of writing.

For them, writing to an acquaintance was an art in itself, and learning how to write a letter was an important part of their education. It wasn't only the form, content, grammar and punctuation of the letter that had to be up to snuff either, but the penmanship itself. Though today some handwriting in letters from the period can be virtually indecipherable, so too can we examine beautifully crafted examples of the art of letter writing from young ladies who were putting everything they'd learned into practice. It was a form of self-expression.

Though creative writing wasn't encouraged, journals and diaries written by women in the eighteenth century have left us with valuable pen portraits of their life and times. From Frances Burney's intimate knowledge of the court of George III and Queen Charlotte during the King's health crises to Anne Lister's intricate coded journals, through their words we are able to relive the times they knew. We see the real women behind the carefully constructed portraits and hear voices that would otherwise have remained silent.

There were some educational subjects that both girls and boys were taught, though generally with completely different intentions when it came to how they would be used. In the case of arithmetic, household management was once again the driving force behind the instruction young ladies received, specifically the knowledge that a wife would one day be required to manage her family accounts. There would be precious little focus on any other area of arithmetic, and a young lady's governesses would drill her in how to balance budgets and manage every element of the domestic account book. Even the highest members of the ton's female coterie would take on this responsibility, for just as a husband's lands or honorariums – *never* his salary if he was a gentleman – brought in the cash, our ladies had to be adept at managing it.

Reading, writing and arithmetic were the three indispensable cornerstones of female education, but a lady couldn't light up a drawing room with a mastery of three topics alone. Alongside these fundamentals were the lady-like endeavours that could be used to sweeten the offer when eligible bachelors such as Anthony Bridgerton stepped out into the world of the marriage mart.

Though George III's predecessors had immigrated from Germany and brought their own German-speaking courtiers and hangers-on with them, French was the language of the European courts. In elite society, French was therefore the language one was expected to learn with the most fluency, and since the German speakers at court had long since passed into history and George III had obeyed his late father's instructions to establish himself as 'an Englishman born and bred', to be fluent in other tongues wasn't a priority. Queen Charlotte herself had submitted enthusiastically to lessons in English when she was a young bride, determined to fit into the middle-class domestic world that her husband was so keen to create. Italian and German were taught to a certain degree, but only so far as a lady might need them to be able to follow entertainments or perform songs in those tongues. While her brothers were studying Latin and Greek, it was a rare young lady indeed who learned these languages; rather, they were reserved for boys about to embark on lives as gentlemen.

Thanks to Queen Charlotte and her daughters lending an extra air of respectability to botany, art and music, these were all attractive propositions, especially since they offered the chance to be taught by some prestigious and therefore expensive names. The natural sciences were commonly taught to young ladies, alongside a basic knowledge of the humanities. However, while girls would learn by rote the important facts when it came to history, geography, literature and the like, they were certainly not expected to question them. Like philosophy or politics, too much interest in these areas was discouraged. As in all things, a good wife should merely facilitate and participate in the discussion; she shouldn't seek to dominate or influence it at the cost of her husband.

Once the vital subjects and conversation topics were out of the way, what remained for girls were the all-important artistic endeavours. Some of these had practical uses too – none more so than needlework. Though the wealthy ladies of the ton certainly wouldn't be making or mending their own clothes, philanthropy was a major occupation in a world where even the Queen once gave away diamonds to a clergyman in need. With the stakes so high, making clothing for charity was something gentlewomen could do to raise their own philanthropic profile among their circle. Needlework served a decorative purpose too, and ladies worked on projects such as embroidery or knotting to give as gifts or display at home. Just as people meet today to knit and natter, Regency women could be glimpsed carrying their work baskets to daily social engagements, where they would occupy their hands while they got down to the serious business of socializing. Particularly canny ladies saved their most impressive projects for these social sewing sessions, using them as one more opportunity to show off their skills and accomplishments to whoever happened to be watching.

With beautiful penmanship taken care of, illustration and painting were next on the slate. Girls were particularly encouraged to master these subjects, and in the case of more wealthy families they trained under household names of the era, such as miniaturist William Marshall Craig and composer Samuel Wesley, who was known as 'the English Mozart'. With women discouraged from engaging in business, an ability to paint and perhaps tutor others in the skill could have a practical use too. Not all women would find a husband, and those who didn't often faced a difficult future. Spinsterhood was considered unnatural, but an upper-class woman working for a living was frowned upon, and any inheritance she might receive would usually be put in trust and placed under the control of a male relative. Because of this, many unmarried women of the upper classes had to rely on their families to keep them. Taking a few young ladies as respectable pupils in artistic lessons was a way of earning just a little bit of money that they could call their own while making use of natural talents. Jane Austen fans have much to be grateful for when it comes to the matter of young ladies mastering art; the only known image of Austen produced during her lifetime was drawn by her sister, Cassandra. Sadly, many talented female painters have been lost to history thanks to the social norms of the day, but there was one particularly remarkable artist who enjoyed enormous fame during the Regency against seemingly insurmountable odds.

Sarah Biffin was born without arms or legs but was able to paint beautiful works using her mouth. She was exhibited across the land to gawking audiences as 'The Limbless Wonder' until George Douglas, Earl of Morton, discovered her remarkable talents and became her patron. Under Morton's patronage Biffin undertook lessons from painter William Marshall Craig and became one of the most celebrated female artists of her day. Her work was shown at the Royal Academy, and the royal family commissioned her to paint miniatures of them, beginning an association that eventually, after some very tough times, led to Biffin receiving a pension courtesy of Queen Victoria in the last years of her life. Her story is deserving of a Netflix series all of its own.

Music was another accomplishment that was seen as vital for a young lady of the ton. When Queen Charlotte was travelling to England as a teenage bride, she had entertained those who shared the voyage with tunes played upon her harpsichord, and she and George III held intimate concerts for friends in the early years of their marriage. In displaying her musical acumen, the young Queen demonstrated one of the most desirable accomplishments for any would-be lady of the ton. Young ladies were taught to sing and play instruments from childhood, both of which were highly desirable qualities when it came to snapping up a suitor. Unlike arithmetic or rote knowledge of history, these artistic endeavours, along with dancing, even gave a rare opportunity to channel a little bit of seduction.

The instruments that respectable women were permitted to play were limited, and any that infringed upon propriety were entirely out of the question. There was to be no blowing anything, nor was there to be too much movement, and certainly no undue excitement. Just as Queen Charlotte had impressed at the harpsichord years earlier, this remained a popular choice, though it began to fall out of favour as time went on and pianos became a staple of every polite household.

Marie Antoinette had been an accomplished harpist, and even more than a decade after her death the harp retained a peculiar mystique for young ladies, but a harp and harp tutor were outside the reach of all but the most privileged. Little wonder that the harp was soon a status symbol all by itself.

When it came to seductive accomplishments, though, nothing beat the dance floor. An ability to dance was absolutely vital if a deb wanted to make a lasting impact in seconds, and in a world where there was no shortage of debs, hitting the dance floor running could make all the difference. There were plenty of rules still to be observed, though, and the first was that a dance was far from a free-for-all. For a start, before a lady could dance with a gentleman, they had to be formally introduced. If this wasn't possible via a family member or similarly respectable acquaintance, the Master of Ceremonies at a dance could be prevailed upon to ensure that she wouldn't be without partners for the duration of the evening. The name of the lady's partner for each dance was written on a dance card which hung from her wrist along with a small pencil, so she could keep her would-be suitors up to date. For the likes of Edwina Sharma, who had no shortage of dance partners, the ballroom was a place of endless possibilities. To be a wallflower would be the ultimate in social death for some of our Regency heroines.

Once one had secured a variety of partners, however, there were still other challenges to negotiate. Chief among them was the fact that an unbetrothed woman simply could not dance with the same man too many times on one night. A single dance was fine, while two suggested that this relationship may one day blossom beyond the dance floor. Two, however, was the limit; any more than that and the lady concerned would attract some very unwanted attention from the tastemakers of her set. Three dances suggested a woman prone to bad behaviour who risked finding herself left off the guest list of subsequent events.

Almack's was home to the great and the good of the *haut ton*, and the spectacle had to be seen to be believed. Overseen by intimidating Lady Patronesses, obtaining an Almack's voucher was a vital step in a young lady's progress towards an advantageous marriage.

Though Regency dances look very coy and prim to our modern eyes, propriety and society were so rigidly controlled that the opportunity to touch or even hold hands was rare enough to be truly savoured. A chaperone was an omnipresent fact of Regency life, but when couples took a turn on the floor their chaperones had no choice but to stand on the sidelines and keep a hawkish eye on proceedings. There was little they could do to overhear the conversations couples might have while dancing, and the electricity that could be conveyed on a dance floor can't be underestimated. From stolen words to the opportunity to actually touch – albeit through a lady's gloves – the dance floor offered an intimacy that was unheard of for unmarried couples in the Regency. An ability to dance could open all sorts of doors that, for most young ladies, would otherwise be forever marked forbidden.

# RACE

One of the aspects of *Bridgerton* that has particularly caught the imagination of viewers is the diversity of its cast. It exists in a world where racial equality is par for the course, but the reality was sadly far different to that fictional ideal.

By the turn of the century, there were approximately 15,000 black people living in England, and this number rose to more than 20,000 during the Regency. Sadly, their lives were rarely comparable to those of *Bridgerton's* Queen Charlotte or the Duke of Hastings. Racism and discrimination was a daily occurrence, and far from becoming leaders of the ton, often it was difficult for people of colour to find jobs at all. Despite this, the situation for black people in the Regency was actually better than it had been even in the recent past. Thanks to fresh rulings in the 1770s, new legislation recognized that slavery did not exist in English or Scottish law, which set an important precedent for enslaved people who found themselves on British soil. It essentially meant that they became free, and slave owners had no legal power to force an enslaved person onto a vessel that would take them away from England. Despite the challenges faced by black people in the United Kingdom, this ruling made it a place that offered a modicum of safety.

Though it was unusual to find people of colour among the ton, several prominent black people became very popular during the Regency. In 1825, actor Ira Aldridge appeared in London to great acclaim, becoming the first African-American actor to achieve recognition overseas. Boxers Tom Molineaux and Bill Richmond drew enormous crowds to their fights, with Richmond even teaching Lord Byron how to throw a punch. Meanwhile, violinist George Bridgetower, a musician of African descent, rose to stardom in London and across Europe thanks to his remarkable talents. His musical education was personally followed by the Prince Regent himself, and Bridgetower impressed Beethoven so much that he dedicated his Violin Sonata No. 9 to the performer.

Unlike *Bridgerton*, however, the truth is that the ton was not a diverse group. Perhaps the closest one might come in reality is the story of Dido Belle, who was the daughter of an enslaved woman and an English gentleman. Dido was raised a gentlewoman by her father's uncle, the Earl of Mansfield, who had ruled that there was no such thing as slavery on English soil. It has been suggested that his familial relationship with Belle did much to sway his opinion on the topic. Dido didn't live to see the Regency, dying in 1804, but her story has been told on stage, screen and in print many times.

Perhaps one of the most headline-grabbing elements of *Bridgerton*'s ensemble was the casting of Golda Rosheuvel, a Guyanese-British actress, as Queen Charlotte of Mecklenburg-Strelitz. The decision excited a lot of debate and reawakened interest in a theory that the Queen may have been England's first, and so far only, Queen of black heritage. The theory was first suggested by historian Mario de Valdes y Cocom, who claims that he is able to trace Charlotte's genealogy back through nine generations to Margarita de Castro y Sousa, a fifteenth-century Portuguese noblewoman who he posits was black. He notes that some accounts of Charlotte's appearance used racially pejorative terms to describe her and points to portraits in which the Queen's complexion is notably darker than that usually seen in eighteenth-century portraiture.

Valdes's research into Queen Charlotte's ancestry has been hotly disputed and challenged by historians, who argue that the nine generations that divide Margarita and Charlotte render such connections moot. Others believe that Valdes may have misinterpreted the historical evidence regarding Margarita's ethnicity, which would obviously have implications for his theories regarding Charlotte's heritage. The British royal household, meanwhile, has no comment to make on the matter.

# LEVELLING UP

Though it wasn't impossible to improve one's social standing, it was difficult. Women could do it through marriage, as proven at the close of the eighteenth century when Elizabeth Farren, the actress daughter of an alcoholic surgeon, wed the 12th Earl of Derby after a courtship that fascinated the chattering classes. Her suitor was Edward Smith-Stanley, whose first marriage had ended after his wife enjoyed a scandalous public affair. The earl refused to divorce his errant wife in order to prevent her from marrying her lover, but when he started courting Elizabeth Farren, his plan backfired. Elizabeth insisted that her mother chaperone them everywhere they went, an arrangement that went on until Lord Stanley was finally widowed. Six weeks after the death of his first wife, the Earl of Derby married Farren.

Nor was social climbing quite as easy as romantic fiction made it look, as the intention of the upper classes was to preserve their estates and consolidate or increase their wealth by making marriages to those of a similar social standing. It wasn't only young ladies looking for dukes, either; plenty of titled young men held themselves out as tempting morsels for the daughters of rich families who would bring with them a very generous dowry. That same dowry could appeal to a higher-status husband fallen on hard times, who would happily bestow his title on a wife in return for her family money. These, of course, were not always the happiest of marriages.

Sometimes, one could start a process that would pay social dividends for the next generation. For instance, a son who went to university would be open to opportunities for networking with the sons of nobility, which might prove beneficial in later years. Even an apprenticeship, like that undertaken by John Soane, could see the apprentice elevated far beyond his origins. Soane was the son of a bricklayer, but his apprenticeship in architecture was the start of a career that eventually saw him appointed clerk of works for St James's Palace and in receipt of a knighthood of his own. Today, he is remembered as a towering figure in the field of Regency architecture.

In general, though, the marriage mart offered the best chance for immediate consolidation or improvement – within reason. We'll look at it in a little more detail later, but before one ventures out to Almack's, it's vital that one knows what to wear – and what not to …

# CHAPTER TWO

# FASHION

'Oh! how I delight in that drapery thin,
That sheweth each muscle that moveth within;
That gossamer dress, which so nicely conceals,
Yet still fires the bosom by what it reveals.'

'A Poetic Epistle', *The Lady's Monthly Museum*[9]

ew things conjure a vision of the Regency quite as freely
as fashion. Though *Bridgerton*'s brightly patterned
Empire-waisted gowns might take some liberties when
it comes to colour and print, they capture that quintessential
silhouette familiar to fans of everything from Jane Austen to
Julia Quinn. Throughout history, fashion has been a language
all of its own, with dress silently saying so much about the
person who wears it. In the Regency it communicated wealth
and status, and in the ton, getting it right was everything.

Obvious to any *Bridgerton* fan, Queen Charlotte of Mecklenburg-Strelitz's fashion tastes were stuck in a previous era as the grand ostentation of the 1700s was replaced by simple Empire-line dresses and elegant, natural hairstyles following the French Revolution.

Nobody who has watched *Bridgerton* can have missed Queen Charlotte's eye-popping wardrobe, nor failed to notice how it jars with the world of fashion over which she presides. Queen Charlotte was a product of a different time and a different court, and throughout her life her wardrobe and attitudes to fashion reflected that. She was born in 1744 to the small ducal court of Mecklenburg-Strelitz, at a time when standards of dress were very different to those of the Regency. Queen Charlotte's wide skirts and powdered wigs were once the height of fashion, but by the time Prinny ruled they were relics of a different era. These relics, however, were preserved in aspic at Charlotte's court, where everyone was expected to follow her lead, and that included the clothes they wore. Queen Charlotte had no truck with modern looks, right down to refusing to allow her ladies to wear towering feathers in their hair as fashion dictated, and of course nobody would ever dream of complaining. Instead, ladies whose wardrobes would usually be the height of modernity clothed themselves in dated court gowns that hid their forms and restricted their movements whenever they were at court, and any frustrations were aired strictly in private. It was a small price to pay for having the ear of the Queen, and there were ample opportunities to indulge one's fashion tastes away from the stuffy world of Queen Charlotte's court.

Fashion in the Regency was unlike anything that had gone before in the United Kingdom. The Age of Enlightenment and the American War of Independence had changed the country forever, and over the sea the French Revolution had fundamentally altered the face of Europe. The face of fashion changed with it. In a world where conspicuous consumption and ostentatious show had been punished by the guillotine, few wanted to be accused of flaunting their wealth.

The eighteenth century had been a time of excess where 'more is more' was the order of the day. Dresses grew wider and ever more elaborate and wigs were commonplace, the more flamboyant the better among the wealthiest classes. As the nineteenth century dawned and those who had led fashion in the eighteenth century grew older, a new generation rose to prominence. This generation eschewed the overblown extravagance of the decades just passed and pursued a simpler line, the better to show off the natural form. The wide panniers, heavy fabrics and ostentatious powdered wigs of their mothers and grandmothers were cast off in favour of aesthetics borrowed from classical antiquity which the Age of Enlightenment had embraced. Waistlines rose higher and simple bonnets rather than wigs concealed hair, while in male and female wardrobes alike rich ornamentation and extravagant textiles were replaced by stark whites or plainer fabrics like cool, lightweight cotton. The male physique became more pronounced in short waistcoats and tight breeches, while the female form was no longer hidden beneath wide skirts and sack-back gowns. By the time the Regency dawned, the high-Georgian 'more is more' look that Queen Charlotte enforced at court was otherwise glimpsed only among those who had simply failed to keep up with changing trends. What had once been a sign of modernity was now a thing of the past.

Members of the ton didn't do fashion by halves, and whether relaxing in the countryside or enjoying the social whirl of the Season, clothing was a language in itself. Ladies snapped up copies of magazines like *Ackermann's Repository of Arts* and *La Belle Assemblée*, in which colour fashion plates showed the most stylish looks to give women ideas to pass on to their dressmakers. Like magazines or even Instagram today, they showed off emerging trends and captured the zeitgeist, and readers lapped it up.

# WHAT THE LADIES WORE

During the Regency, the formality of one's dress was described in one of three ways: undress, half dress and full dress. Each of these was distinctly different both in its style and in the circumstances where it would be worn. Getting it right was an essential part of survival at the top of the ton. One wrong move and questions would be asked!

Undress wasn't naked or even underwear, but casual. It was the dress a lady would wear in the morning, or perhaps even later if she didn't have any engagements that demanded her to look her best. Undress was for around the house and was intended to be comfortable and relatively laid-back. It certainly didn't do to be seen in undress by anyone other than one's closest acquaintances.

The next stage was known as half dress. Not quite casual but not as showy as full dress, half dress was a little more formal than the former but less so than the latter. Basically, it was the equivalent of what we might describe today as smart casual. Half dress was for friends and calls where a lady wanted to make an effort without trying too hard. After all, we wouldn't meet for coffee wearing a sequinned cocktail frock … maybe.

Full dress was an opportunity to wear the most sumptuous gowns in a woman's wardrobe as they clothed themselves in the finest fabrics and most delicate needlework money could buy. The *Bridgerton* taste for rich, colourful fabrics, though, was not so popular, with most women likely to plump for demure pastel shades.

Last but very definitely not least was full dress, which was the highest level of formality in Regency dress. Full dress was reserved for strictly formal occasions such as elite events, balls and court. Dressing in anything less than the best when full dress was required was a major social faux pas and not something any conscientious member of the ton would be caught doing.

Dressing in the Regency era was a serious business, and for tastemakers virtually a full-time job. From tightening stays to dampening cotton gowns so that they might stick to a girl's curves, there are plenty of myths about ladies' fashion from the time. Perhaps the easiest way to separate fact from fiction is to establish what the types of dress consisted of, then to look at what it took to dress a lady from the bottom layer out.

The clothing a woman wore was dictated by what her diary contained each day. Upon rising, she would put on her morning dress, and which morning dress was chosen would depend on whether she was spending the morning indoors or taking a social stroll. An indoor morning dress was a simple, very comfortable white gown. It was a dress to be worn in private, and certainly not for greeting any but the most intimate visitors. A married woman would likely conceal her hair in a bun beneath a similarly simple cap while taking care of her domestic business: this was no time for frivolity. If a woman was heading out for a stroll, however, it was all about keeping up with her neighbours. Promenading was a serious business for the queens of fashion and a chance to be seen in the newest, most on-trend looks, ornamented with a parasol in fine weather or a fan that could sometimes be used as a language all of its own. When one went out and about, there was always the chance that one might be seen.

Afternoons were usually the time when social calls were made, and a lady would be sure to have changed out of her informal morning dress to receive her visitors or make calls of her own. She would still be relatively casual for friends, though her dress would be fashionable and likely considered as afternoon half dress. A dress worn for promenading in town would also be suitable for receiving visitors without making it look like too much of an effort was being made to show off. It wouldn't do to be labelled a try-hard, after all!

Half dress was the next step up in terms of formality and ornamentation, sitting as it did between afternoon walking gowns and evening full dress. Half dress was usually worn as the afternoon slipped into the evening, but no later than that if a lady was heading out for the night. Necklines were lower and caps were cast off in favour of fashionable hairstyles – of which, more later – or perhaps even an ornamented bandeau. Half dress textiles were notably richer than those used in undress clothing but stopped short of the very best, which was reserved for full dress. Just as more decolletage made an appearance as the day turned into night, short sleeves and gloves were an essential part of the evening look. One might very occasionally attend an event in half dress, but only rarely; instead, there was the option of half full dress, which hovered right on the edge of the most showy gowns in the wardrobe. While a lady might pop to the pleasure gardens so attired, she wouldn't dream of setting foot in Almack's.

The chance to really pull out all the stops came when a lady's maid helped her mistress into full dress. When *Bridgerton* viewers think of those most showy, bejewelled gowns that sparkle in the light of dazzling chandeliers, they're most likely conjuring images of full dress. And what images they are.

Other than the formalities of court dress, it didn't get any showier than full dress, and there was no better opportunity to show off one's wealth and good taste. Full dress echoed the same basic shape of the rest of the female Regency wardrobe, namely a slender silhouette with an Empire waistline which sat just beneath the bust, but the textiles and ornamentation would be much finer than those of other gowns. What we know as the Empire style was referred to at the time as Directoire, a reference to the fashion looks emerging from Napoleonic France, where high waistlines and loose skirts were enormously fashionable thanks to their being championed by Empress Joséphine, one of the tastemakers of her age. The comfortable cotton of morning gowns was nowhere to be seen in full dress. Instead, ladies were clad in crêpe or satin, overlaid with the likes of lace and gossamer to create a shimmering, opulent look.

Though Bridgertonians have fallen in love with the beautiful bright dresses worn in the show, they wouldn't have been found in many Regency wardrobes. Instead, gowns were generally white or solid pastel shades, with the most extravagant colours reserved for trimmings and accessories. Those trimmings might on occasion include a train, but more commonly a hemline would be high enough to allow for dancing, and shoes were usually delicate slippers in which a lady could take a turn on the floor. These were a world apart from the brocaded heels worn at the height of the Georgian period and have caused many a fictional Regency heroine to fall afoul of a rainstorm. But dancing was the order of the day in the marriage mart, and slippers were practically obligatory; after all, with dancing came intrigue, and what could be better for a ton tastemaker?

When a lady was in full dress, she was never without her pristine gloves. The neat caps of daytime were replaced by headdresses such as bandeaus or turbans, which might be ornamented with the kind of elaborate feathers Queen Charlotte absolutely hated. A woman in full dress was never seen without her jewellery, either, which was another opportunity to demonstrate the family wealth and, for the single gal in search of a husband, the sort of dowry she might be able to bring into a marriage.

Finally, in a class of its own was court dress. Court dress adhered to a set of very strict rules and was quite unsuitable for wearing anywhere else thanks to its extreme formality and the fact that it was hugely unfashionable by the time the Regency rolled around. As mentioned previously, though the Prince Regent revelled in fashion, while Queen Charlotte presided over the court there was little concession to such trivialities. The ladies who appeared at court were the pinnacle of polite society and understood intrinsically that the dress rules set by the old Queen were rigid and not to be trifled with.

While fashions were revolutionizing towards more modest, understated silhouettes in much of Regency society, Queen Charlotte's court remained steadfast in its preference for wide, hooped skirts. The result, when women of fashion attempted to combine the two styles, was a ridiculous shape bringing high Empire waistlines together with expansive skirts just below the bust.

Court dress was unpractical and unwieldy and had barely changed in generations. Though the panniers Charlotte wears in *Bridgerton*, which widened the hips to sometimes absurd proportions while keeping the front and back of the gown flat, had not been worn at court for years, nor were fashionable column dresses allowed either. Instead, court dress consisted of skirts with trains and an underlayer of hoops that disguised the form beneath. When ladies attempted to combine this with a modern high-waisted design, they were left with an extremely odd-looking cut-and-shut of a dress, which was modern on top and utterly out of date on the bottom. Though the Queen loathed tall feathers atop the head, she was happy to continue the old tradition of white plumes in the hair. These plumes gradually crept higher and higher until a well-placed word from the Queen or one of her trusted circle brought them back down to a more traditional length.

By the time the King withdrew from public life, the incoming Regent's marriage had already collapsed in spectacularly public fashion. Though he was still married to Caroline of Brunswick, the couple were living totally separate lives, so she never had the opportunity to stamp her unconventional influence on the court. She would later utterly scandalize polite society by flashing her knees and dancing in diaphanous gowns with nothing underneath while on the Continent, but the British court certainly didn't witness such scenes. Instead, Queen Charlotte continued to rule to roost, and on the matter of court dress she was utterly immovable.

The Prince Regent and his mother had had some spectacular fallings-out in the past, but as Charlotte grew older and her husband's illness left her more isolated, she and Prinny became each other's strongest supporters. Though the Regent was a man of fashion and a tastemaker extraordinaire, he still knew better than to meddle in the court dress that his mother controlled so tightly. Only when the old King and Queen were dead and Prinny ruled as King George IV did he allow the ladies of the court to change the style that had been set in stone for decades. Hoops were finally set aside in favour of more simple and fashionable dresses, and the elaborate feathered headdresses that had been forbidden now became de rigueur. Though the tradition for ostrich feathers continued, they were incorporated into ever more fanciful and showy headpieces until swathes of feathers floated in the breeze high above the heads of the queens of the ton. Queen Charlotte would have reached for her smelling salts had she been around to witness such decadence.

Before we move on to the gentlemen, this is an opportune moment to go through the layers of clothing a lady would wear one at a time. It's also a chance to dispel some myths, namely that of torturous, tight-laced corsets. If these ever existed at all, they certainly weren't a part of life in the Regency, though *Bridgerton* viewers could be forgiven for thinking otherwise, having watched scenes of eye-watering tight-lacing in the show.

Contrary to popular belief, corsets weren't the first layer and certainly never sat directly against the skin. Instead, the base layer was the chemise, or shift, which was a simple linen garment that skimmed the mid-calf in order to ensure no accidental flashes of skin. Only then were the stays put on, and they weren't showy, tightly laced garments either. In fact, they were plain linen, shaped only lightly with bone and a rigid busk that ran down the front, and fastened with laces down the back. Though the prevailing myth is that stays were painful and restricting, that generally wasn't the case. The main restriction came around the shoulders, where straps made it a challenge to fully lift the arms. Apart from this, Regency stays were comfortable to wear … there was certainly no need to grab on to the bedpost and grit your teeth like Scarlett O'Hara.

Once the shift and stays were in place, then came the stockings, held by garters. Once again these weren't ornate and were meant to be functional rather than fancy. A lady topped up her under-layers with a simple petticoat, which covered from the neckline of her gown to the lower leg. So they wouldn't disrupt the line of a gown, they were usually high-waisted, essentially mirroring the shape of the outer-layers and dispelling myths that gowns were dampened so they clung to the female form beneath. With multiple layers being worn under dresses, all a dampened lady would achieve was discomfort; she certainly wouldn't be firing her best come-hither look at every eligible bachelor who crossed her path.

You may notice one thing missing from this list of underwear, and that, of course, is drawers. That isn't a mistake, because in the vast majority of cases a lady wouldn't be wearing them. Drawers weren't common in the Regency era at all, and weren't part of the rather comprehensive underwear layers worn by upper-class women of the time.

Atop all these under-layers came the gown, then whatever shawl, pelisse, spencer or other outer-layers were required. As you can imagine, Regency dress provided a freedom of movement that was entirely new to women. Gone were the heavy petticoats and hoops or panniers of earlier generations, and the hitherto hidden feminine shape was easy to discern through light dresses, even with all those layers beneath. But the world of the ton didn't turn on women alone, and those showy balls would have been rather one-sided affairs if there were no men present to squire the ladies around the floor.

# WHAT THE GENTS WORE

In the eighteenth century, male fashion had been for ornate, intricately embroidered pieces, with knee breeches, stockings and buckled shoes the go-to for the fashionable man about town. In the Regency, however, those elaborate looks were yesterday's news, and just as ladies took their cues from classical antiquity and turned to simple columns of white, men found inspiration from similar sources. For decades, a rite of passage for young men had been the Grand Tour, an opportunity to explore Europe and take in the great historical sites of interest. As Colin Bridgerton learned, the Grand Tour offered an opportunity to immerse oneself not only in wine, women and song but in the remains of the classical world, from exquisite marbles to frescoes that had existed since ancient times. Those works, with their emphases on the perfect muscular form, made an impact on the men who saw them and the fashionable wardrobes that emerged as the years passed.

Once upon a time, wealth had been signified by the showy textiles and embellishments that men employed in their clothing. Lace and embroidery were as commonplace in male clothes as female, but as the eighteenth century ticked over into the nineteenth, the cut and tailoring of a suit replaced brocade, velvet and lace as an indicator of wealth and quality. Knee breeches grew longer and trousers more commonplace, while the oceans of silk and lace that once encircled shirt cuffs were gone. In fact, all those heavy, stiff fabrics were given the heave-ho, replaced by wool and cotton or hard-wearing buckskin for that iconic Mr Darcy look.

*'The Dandy from his chamber stalks,*
*To take his morning lounge and walks,*
*And after lounging up and down*
*In Dandy stile, through Southwark town,*
*He cross'd the water in a wherry,*
*Walk'd up Size Lane to Bucklersbury.'*[10]

Beau Brummell was the most famous of all the dandies,
with his preference for muted colours and precise tailoring
influencing men's fashion even into the twenty-first century.

This revolution in men's fashion owed its existence in large
part to the dandy, who emerged in the last years of the

eighteenth century. Perhaps the most famous dandy, and certainly the most influential, was Beau Brummell, "'the glass of fashion"in St. James's-street', who held himself and his fashionable set, of which the Regent was a leading member, to the highest personal standards.[11] The perfectly tailored yet sober garments espoused by Brummell were an explicit rejection of the ostentatious styles that had been worn by the previous generation. To be a dandy was to show one's sense not only of style but of taste in all things.

Though *Bridgerton* fans are already more than familiar with exactly what lay under those clothes, it's worth going layer by layer just as we did with our gentlewoman above. You may recall that she had three layers before she even got to her gown, but things were a little simpler for the gentleman about town.

When it came to underwear, there were two options. Some gents wore drawers, which were very similar in cut to a pair of breeches. They fastened with buttons and were tight enough not to cause any bagginess beneath a pair of fashionable unmentionables. For those who preferred not to wear drawers, the other option was to pull the shirt tails up into something resembling a Regency nappy. Not quite how fans might picture the Duke of Hastings, but that was just the way things were done. A pair of plain stockings completed the undergarments, unless a chap felt he needed stays. Few admitted it if they did, but there were certainly eyebrows raised about what might be going on under the corpulent Prince Regent's blinged up military tunics.

Essentially, that was it, so if our gent eschewed drawers in favour of shirt tails he was already partially in his outerwear. Though book covers showing rippling abs beneath unbuttoned flouncy shirts may sometimes suggest otherwise, Regency shirts didn't fasten from top to bottom but only from the neck to around the middle of the chest. The shirt was fastened with buttons that would be concealed beneath a cravat and ended in plain cuffs of a couple of inches or so, with none of the fancy lace that would have been a signifier of wealth and taste just a few years earlier. The sleeves, however, were where just a little indulgence was allowed, made out of voluminous amounts of linen which was pleated and gathered at the shoulder and cuff. In full dress, a gent was also allowed a little more flounce when it came to his shirt front and might add a few frills when he was dressed for best.

Next came the 'unmentionables', or breeches. Knee breeches and silk stockings were in their death throes by the time the Regency began, favoured only by those who were stuck in an earlier time. Though Regency gents preferred fitted trousers in town and when wearing full or half dress, buckskin breeches have become synonymous with the period thanks to plenty of Regency-set fiction. The familiar buff buckskin was still commonplace while in the country or if a more casual look was the order of the day. It was also a surprising symbol of wealth: as buckskin couldn't be laundered and would eventually go out of shape, breeches had to be replaced often, something only a chap with money at his disposal could afford to do. Regardless of the style, though, unmentionables were tight-fitting and intended to draw attention to the male shape just as the female shape was revealed by the Empire waist and low-cut necklines that fashion dictated. If a gent's musculature wasn't quite up to what he considered to be an acceptable standard, a little padding might be employed, but this would be done sparingly. Rumours of heavily padded calves are, rather sadly, just that. The breeches were held up with braces and opened with a flap at the front, known as the front fall. The fall could be broad or narrow, but in all cases it buttoned shut to spare our gentleman's blushes.

Once the gent was in his basic look, it was time to add the finishing touches. A waistcoat offered a chance to show a little flair, and many were ornately decorated, especially for important occasions. Unlike modern examples, Regency waistcoats were entirely flat across the bottom, rather than tapered. They were tightened at the back by buckled straps or ties, but that was something a gentleman's valet would take care of. The valet might also take care of the cravat, which had to be starched if one wanted to be a true dandy. Though Brummell and his set favoured a pristine white cravat, a brightly coloured Belcher cravat offered the option to go as flamboyant as you liked in an otherwise sober look.

Sober was certainly the order of the day for the obligatory

gentleman's coat. Once again, the coat was tailored to show off the physique, especially in its tailed appearance, which dropped to the thighs at the back while being cut to just above the waist at the front, thus showcasing a glimpse of the waistcoat beneath. Once the coat would have been embroidered and decorated as a mark of status, but by the Regency less was more. One of the few concessions was the fashion for gold buttons on a blue coat, but this was the only exception to an otherwise relatively staid rule.

Next came the boots, which existed in various lengths depending on the activity our gent was undertaking and how much of his impressive calves he hoped to show off. Alternatively, shoes were plain leather and fastened with a buckle; once again, flamboyance was the last thing he wanted to be accused of. A gentlemen finished off the look with a pair of buff gloves and a beaver hat if outdoors, then he was ready to promenade and catch the eye of whichever girls happened to be passing!

When it came to court dress, of course, once again fashion came second to tradition. In keeping with the Queen's wishes, men wore formal suits in dark fabric ornamented with intricate embroidery and the sort of lace one would never see out in the street in those modern times. Knee breeches and silk stockings were part of the uniform, as was a ceremonial sword. In fact, images showing courtiers of the Regency era are barely discernible from those of the previous generation. In some things, progress was going at a snail's pace.

# HAIRDOS AND DON'TS

The Regency era was one typified by neoclassical influences. With fashionistas taking inspiration from the statues and drawings of the ancient world and hoping to present a more natural look, it was inevitable that their crowning glories would soon undergo the same revision as their wardrobes. As styles evolved, wigs that required architectural underpinnings were abandoned in favour of hairdos, such as the Apollo or the Cirque knot, that were simple, casual styles designed to make the best of the natural hair without the need for scaffolding, powder and horsehair. Once upon a time wigs had swept hair back, away from the face and concealed it, but during the Regency curls that framed the face were the done thing. Far from the formality of the Georgian era, loose buns worn at the back of the head kept tresses neatly stowed, once again putting natural looks to the fore. Despite this, women were rarely, if ever, seen in public with their hair free after childhood, and completely undressed hair was reserved for the most intimate private settings. Married women always wore their hair up when in public, never loose.

Gone were the fruit baskets, botanical displays and galleons that dressed fashionable styles in decades before, replaced by pretty ribbons such as those beloved of Lydia Bennet, while pearls, ornamented combs and simple flowers were added to create a showier style. Just like dress, hair would be changed depending on the time of day. For instance, in the morning the hair would be fastened beneath a cap or tied in a bandeau, while it would be ornamented though still natural for evening occasions. Like all things, the more elaborate of these ornaments were intended to show off a family's wealth without doing so ostentatiously. False hairpieces could be added if necessary, though these were always integrated into the real hair, as opposed to worn like an obvious wig. Queen Charlotte herself had enhanced her natural barnet with coronation locks – hair extensions – at her husband's coronation half a century earlier.

With the French Revolution much too close for comfort, English fashions changed dramatically in just a few years, with the emphasis tending towards modest, natural hairstyles. Gone forever were the enormous wigs of just a generation before – and in France some women even began to wear a choppy, early pixie-cut style, reflecting those killed by Madame La Guillotine.

In years past, one would look for a very long time to find a lady who had cut her hair short, but such styles also began to flourish in the early nineteenth century. Like the Directoire dress style that crossed the Channel from France, a fashion for radically different haircuts also reached England from her continental neighbour in the wake of the French Revolution.

When the Reign of Terror ended, a subculture of young people emerged who had lost friends, family and fortunes to the National Razor. These tastemakers held events called *bals des victimes*, exclusive social gatherings that honoured the victims of the revolution in a darkly irreverent way. Attendees greeted one another by giving a violent jerk of their head, while women wore narrow red-ribbon chokers to suggest the cut of the guillotine, draping themselves in red shawls that called to mind Charlotte Corday when she was put to death for the murder of revolutionary leader Jean-Paul Marat. Most influential, however, was the *coiffure à la victime*, a short, cropped hairstyle that mimicked that forced upon prisoners immediately before they were beheaded. It was a radical look and one that symbolized a follower of fashion at the very cutting edge – no pun intended.

The highly fashionable and notorious Lady Caroline Lamb wore a short bob that influenced more daring ladies to follow suit, but by far the most popular style was that familiar to many from modern Jane Austen adaptations, with the hair fastened up and ringlets framing the face. These curls would be teased forward to peep out from beneath a cap, bandeau or bonnet during the day, even though bonnets are rare sights indeed in the world of *Bridgerton*. It became desirable to keep the back of the neck uncovered, as a pretty neck was considered one of the best assets a woman possessed – or at least one of the best assets she was permitted to show in polite society!

For men as well as women, hair powder fell out of favour and natural hair colour was allowed to shine through. This was helped along by practical considerations, as Prime Minister William Pitt the Younger's tax on hair powder in the late 1700s caused an outcry among fashionable men. With flour hard to get, they rebelled by wearing wigs in their natural hair colour, which they eventually cast off in favour of simply wearing no wigs at all. At the forefront of the rebellion was the Duke of Bedford, who threw off his wig and proudly wore a highly fashionable waxed crop style instead. Though some professions still required wigs to be worn, the only place where they remained common was at court, where men were expected to follow the same outdated traditions that saw them in silk stockings while the ladies wore hooped skirts and flopping ostrich feathers.

Though some more traditional gentlemen held on to their wigs to the last, for the most part men followed women, taking their lead on styles from antiquity. Names emerged from ancient Rome and Greece, popularizing such looks as the *Titus*, the *Caesar* and the *Brutus*, the latter made famous by Beau Brummell. Hair was styled with wax or a pomade made of rendered bear fat and washed as infrequently as possible. Regency gents grew their hair longer than previous generations and brushed it forwards, growing long sideburns that framed the face just as ringlets framed the faces of women. Though sideburns were fashionable, men about town were otherwise clean-shaven, leaving facial hair to those who were a long, long way from the ton.

# MAKE-UP ...
# THE NATURAL WAY

To make a splash in the ton, one had to look the part. A lady assembled a wardrobe to envy, made sure her hair was just so and added her best jewellery to showcase her family's prestige. Before she slipped on her gloves, though, there was still one last finishing touch: make-up. Not so many years before the Regency, make-up was common in the upper classes for both men and women, and a pale face accented by red lips and rouged cheeks was the order of the day; a nude palette was definitely not the Georgian look. In fact, some women's adherence to fashion was also their downfall, thanks to the dangerous compounds used in some products.

The celebrated Maria Gunning, Countess of Coventry, and her sworn rival, courtesan Kitty Fisher, were both famed for their whiter than white complexions. Those complexions were achieved with liberal applications of a cosmetic that contained white lead. When the two women died, many commentators attributed their youthful demises to lead poisoning, contracted from the make-up they wore.

Thankfully, by the time of the Regency, fashions had changed. In concert with the move towards more natural hair and less restrictive dress, so too was make-up becoming something that enhanced natural features, rather than painted them out. Just as clothing had become less flamboyant, the move to a more natural complexion reflected the swerve away from ostentation in the wake of the French Revolution. Now if one were to be on-trend, it was all about respectability, and that meant a pale, flawless complexion with a healthy, rosy glow. 'More is more' was now the mark of vulgarity, and that was something the ton abhorred.

> *Cleanliness is of most powerful efficacy. It maintains the limbs in their pliancy; the skin in its softness; the complexion in its lustre; the eyes in their brightness; the teeth in their purity; and the constitution in its fairest vigour.*[12]

Perhaps mindful of the rumoured ravages of white lead, which was by now known to be 'ruinous to health (occasioning paralytic affections and premature death)',[13] ladies were spending more time than ever caring for their skin, rather than clogging it up. Toners containing ambergris and vinegar promised to bring a lustre to the face and could be easily cooked up at home using recipes taken from the indispensable *Mirror of the Graces* – or more affordable options might include lavender or rose water.

*The Mirror of the Graces*, published in 1811, was a how-to guide for the Regency lady. It offered advice on fashion, cosmetics and other aspects of genteel life from an anonymous author who claimed to have mingled with the highest ranks of society, both in the UK and across the Continent. The book emphasized the idea that a woman's outward appearance was a reflection of her character and personality and encouraged the virtues of smooth skin, tidy hair and delicate conversation. In pursuit of perfection, members of the ton splashed on skin lotions with such OTT names as Olympian Dew, itself a nod to ancient Greece, while those a little lower down the ladder could buy copies of exclusive lotions in much the same way that dupes of luxury bags and shoes are sold in their thousands across the world today. Of course, one must always be on the lookout for mercury as an ingredient, because beauty at the cost of health and life was a price nobody should have to pay.

For the most picky ladies, or those who couldn't get to shops that sold commercially produced products, there was always the option to make your own or have your lady's maid do it for you. Crushing up fruits or cucumber became an everyday pastime for some and a job for others who were hoping to find a more natural or affordable solution to add a glow to their cheeks and a softness to their skin.

Of course, the make-up rules we're about to learn weren't universal to all women, but any fashionable young lady would be sure to follow trends. More mature women had never known a time when natural was the way to go, and some found the change in habits a little difficult to swallow, just as some people today stick to the styles that were popular and flattered them in their youth. That's why you may on rare occasions see portraits from the Regency era that depict mature women in the stark white powder and red rouge of a generation past.

*No eye that is of the commonest apprehension can look on a face bedaubed with white paint, pearl powder, or enamel, and be deceived for a minute into a belief that so inanimate a 'whited wall' is the human skin.*[14]

The cosmetics used by Regency women were positively sparse compared to those of a generation earlier, and if one saw a whitened face while the Regent reigned, it would be on a lady who was resisting change as hard as her bewigged male counterpart. Instead, women began to use the forerunners of today's tinted foundations to even out their complexions while retaining a natural look. These foundations were made of crushed white pigments such as cornstarch or pearl, though even with the toxicity of lead now well known, it wasn't entirely out of use. Likewise, a paper disc could be purchased that would be lightly dampened and used as a foundation cake, and these pigments could be given a hint of colour by the addition of a colouring agent such as carmine.

With the face and neck suitably but, the girls hoped, naturally pale, it was time to add some rouge. But not too much. Mindful that 'a violently rouged woman is one of the most disgusting objects to the eye',[15] a mere touch of powder rouge to the cheeks might bring the required glow, as did a dampened rouge cake or even a pomade made from melted wax or fats! Once again, keeping it natural was the aim, so if things glowed a little too much, a light dusting of talcum powder could be used to take out the colour until it was more in keeping with fashion.

Although it was no longer necessary to be as white as alabaster, it was still not done to be tanned or to show off freckles from basking in the sun, both of which would be considered far too earthy. To protect their skin, Regency women turned to a paste known as fard, which was made from almond oil and spermaceti, a waxy substance derived from whales that was used in a variety of cosmetics. These two ingredients were melted together, then honey was added to the cooled paste to create fard. Applied liberally to the skin, it made for a soft complexion and helped avoid sunburn.

If it was too late to avoid the sun, an unction such as Pomade de Seville saw a mixture of lemon juice and egg whites heated over a gentle fire to create a potion that would hopefully take the burn and shine off. Where unfashionable freckles were a recurrent problem, ladies splashed on potions including Unction de Maintenon, which was named after Madame de Maintenon, the secret wife of King Louis XIV. This ointment contained ingredients including lemon juice and oil of tartar and promised to rid the skin of freckles once and for all.

Classical antiquity wasn't the only source of inspiration for the ladies of the ton. Egypt-mania was sweeping the Continent and bringing with it new make-up looks, such as the popularizing of eyeliner and mascara, though eye make-up was really reserved for those who wanted to be a little edgier. Burnt cork made for a pungent but effective pigment, which could add a little hint of darkness to the brows or lashes. But in a world where looking natural was the height of fashion, cat's eyes weren't exactly in keeping with the prevailing tastes. Instead, all that a respectable young lady might hope to get away with would be a very little touch of powder on the eyelids to make her eyes shine. Eyebrows were rarely plucked, though unsightly hairs would certainly be removed so long as it wasn't too obvious. Above all, though, it had to be a nude palette, so nobody would guess there was any make-up there at all.

Though our ladies might not be able to showcase their eyes via cosmetic means, fashion didn't frown quite so much when it came to lip colour ... within reason. Lip colours in the Regency were generally wax-based, coloured with the likes of alkanet and applied like a rouge rather than a lipstick. Alkanet coloured with carmine gave a more subtle, natural colour than the bright red offered by vermilion and produced a complexion more in keeping with the fashion for all things simple.

Just a few years earlier, beauty patches, powdered wigs and opulence in everything had been the mark of money, rank and privilege. But in the shadow the guillotine, less was suddenly very much more.

# CHAPTER THREE

# TRAVEL

**'The finest sight in the metropolis is that of the Mail Coaches setting off from Piccadilly. The horses paw the ground, and are impatient to be gone, as if conscious of the precious burden they convey.'**

William Hazlitt, *The Letter Bell*[16]

For the ton, life was all about seeing and being seen in the right places. Whether in London, aka *in town*, at the country pile or perhaps taking the waters in Bath, it was a constant round of social engagements, making visits and being sure to be in the right place at the right – and most fashionable – time. But of course, with no motorways or train lines to get our tastemakers around, travel took some considerable planning and carried with it considerable risks. Yet these were risks one had to take: with country residences to run, the elite couldn't stay in London forever, after all.

Just like today, different situations called for different types of vehicle, and different vehicles denoted different rungs on the social ladder. From a fashionable young gentleman bombing around town in his phaeton just like a guy in a flashy sports car today, to stately coaches carrying the cream of society to their country estates as though they were in modern Chelsea tractors, vehicles were status symbols that everyone understood.

And not just to show off one's top-of-the-range coach and horses, travel across distances was part of life for the ton, whose diaries bulged with house parties, weekends away and social engagements that couldn't always be held just a short hop across London. At the wealthiest end of the scale, a family coach would undertake the journey using teams of horses, thus avoiding prolonged rest stops. Instead, fresh steeds would be sent on ahead to be changed at posting inns on pre-designated stops along the road. Indeed, for nobles who often had to journey from their estates to London, multiple sets of horses would be permanently boarded along the route since it was such a regular occurrence.

The speed of travel would of course depend on the number of horses pulling the vehicle and the weight it was carrying too. Even 10 miles per hour was outside the reach of most travellers, and with an optimum travel time of roughly 50 or so miles per day, you can imagine how long a journey could take. It was necessary to change the horses approximately every 15 miles, meaning that a journey which today might take ninety minutes would be a considerably more serious undertaking. A jaunt from London to Bath was a weekend away in itself before the spa even came into view.

# GETTING AROUND

A carriage was a considerable expense, and wealthier families had their vehicles custom-built to match their exact requirements. Because this wasn't within everybody's reach, some families were able to purchase second-hand models that would get them around at a fraction of the expense of a custom build. Not only was there the cost of the carriage to think about but that of the horses that would pull it, and the more teams of horses a family had, the more they had to pony up – pun intended – for the privilege.

For those who didn't have the money to maintain multiple parties of horses, the only option on long journeys was to make stops whenever the carriage horses needed to rest. This is where coaching inns were an absolute necessity. The service stations of their day, they offered rest and refreshments for everyone from passengers to footmen to horses too. Additional horses could be rented to take the carriage further along the road, thus hopefully cutting down on waiting time, but all of it cost money that many people simply didn't have. Publications such as *Paterson's British Itinerary* were an invaluable handbook for travellers, listing coach times, posting inns, the distances between locations and other points of interest, including historical sites and unmissable opportunities for sightseeing. Unlike these days of motorways and satellite navigation, planning a trip in the Regency was no easy task.

Public transport over long distances was offered by a variety of providers, one of which was the Royal Mail. The mail coach ran on designated routes every day of the week other than Sunday and religious holidays, carrying post around the country. People were welcome to buy passage on the coach, but they were very definitely second class to the post. Brief stops to change horses offered little chance for respite, as these finely tuned operations switched their steeds and were off again at lightning speed. Passengers who dared to disembark to stretch their legs had to make sure they were back in their seats before the coach set off again, or they'd be left behind. It was a gruelling experience, and a punishing journey on the mail coach left Samuel Taylor Coleridge so 'coach-fevered, coach-crazed and coach-stunn'd' that he had to spend the whole of the next day in bed. This was no first-class experience.

Despite the discomfort, the speed of the mail coach meant that it wasn't a cheap option – but it had some benefits to recommend it. Since stagecoaches could be so overladen with people and cargo that they were cramped and dangerously at risk of overturning, travelling by mail coach frequently offered a more roomy and relatively comfortable option for passengers who could afford to pay a little extra. If travellers were tardy sorts, though, they would have been better to look elsewhere. Whatever happened, the mail must get through, and more than one lackadaisical passenger must have been late returning from a comfort break only to see the coach and their luggage rattling off over the horizon!

A stagecoach stopped outside a wayside inn. If you could afford it, paying extra to travel in this way was eminently worth it, with comfort stops scheduled into the journey. But that was where the comfort ended for most, with poorer passengers squashed onto the top of the coach or even forced to share their spaces with livestock.

An option for cheaper travel existed with stagecoaches. Unlike mail coaches, stagecoaches existed to transport people and cargo rather than to carry post, so though the roads were just as bumpy, rest stops were more generous. Six passengers piled into the cramped interior with as much luggage as could be crammed in alongside them, and they counted themselves lucky to have a seat at all. No doubt they hoped that their fellow travellers both looked after their personal hygiene and didn't try to spread out into more than their fair share of the limited space.

Stagecoaches offered precious little room inside (with what space there was sometimes shared by livestock), so passengers were grateful for the regular rest stops the vehicles made. Coaching inns allowed travellers the chance to rest from the travails of the journey for as long as it took to stretch their legs, grab a snack and take a comfort break. Comfort, however, wasn't open to those who snapped up the very cheapest rides. So long as the horses could carry the load, once the coach was full then places might be offered on top of the vehicle for truly desperate travellers, who braved the trip without handrails, seats or anything to keep them onboard but willpower. The number of people who were crowded onto the roof depended on the amount of baggage that was being transported, but it was really the cheapest – not to mention the most hazardous – option available. Those who had no choice but to cling to the roof hoped for good weather, because come rain, shine or snow, the coach kept on rolling as long as the road could still be travelled.

Of course, the ton would never have need to travel by mail or stagecoach. Instead, they and their households would move between locations in style, sending staff on ahead of time if required, to ensure everything was perfect for their arrival. With bursting wardrobes containing the multiple changes of clothes that fashion dictated, a simple travelling trunk was never going to cut the mustard, so baggage coaches would go on ahead, carrying everything needed for a successful stay. In the case of journeys involving overnight stops on the road, another baggage coach might travel along behind the family, carrying the overnight bags required by the ton. And rest assured, this was more than a rucksack or two.

The roads themselves were a long, long way from the smooth, wide expanses we are so familiar with today, and in a time when each parish was responsible for the upkeep of its own highways and byways, one might find oneself travelling on anything from a well-maintained thoroughfare to a pitted, muddy track. John McAdam's pioneering 'macadam' method of roadbuilding was still a little way off by the Regency, and strapped-for-cash parishes established turnpike trusts, which raised money to improve highways and roads. These were tolls charged to carriage owners in order to use the road; only once the money had been handed over was the turnpike – a toll gate – opened to let a vehicle pass. The money raised then paid for the specific stretch of road that was being tolled, and so on along the road network.

While Georgian roads were often abysmal, the system of turnpikes brought money flooding into the coffers of parishes that were in charge of major routes. This money was ploughed back into improvements on a continual basis, bringing more travellers along to pay a toll to use these well-maintained roads. Despite these improvements, though, travelling any long distance could be harrowing for all sorts of reasons, from bad weather to bad roads to plain old bad people too.

When we think of travelling in the long eighteenth century, the feared figure of the highwayman is never far away. He has been everything from a romantic hero to a notorious criminal, but the glamorous character from fiction was usually anything but desirable or exciting in reality. Instead, highway robbery was a fact of life throughout the Georgian era, and though the risks had reduced significantly by the Regency it was still a hazard of long-distance coach travel, especially along popular routes where the probability of heavy traffic – and more victims – was likely. Mail coaches always had security on board, with an armed guard posted on the rear of the vehicle, ready to intervene if the worst happened.

The possibility of robbery was one reason why a respectable lady would never, ever travel alone. She would be accompanied by a female relative on short journeys for the sake of propriety, but any trip that might bring with it the risk of robbery would only happen with both a chaperone and a man who would take care of trouble should the coach encounter it.

# IN THE SADDLE AND ON FOOT

'Yesterday, had it not been for the dust, might be called the most agreeable of the Season. The Park was crowded even to an excess. The promenade along the foot-path, parallel with Rotten Row, exhibited many thousand well dressed females, with their beaux ... All the fashion and beauty of the metropolis were assembled together about four o'clock; at five, Kensington Gardens were crammed. The Summer attire of our *belles* displayed all the varieties in colour and form of that capricious goddess, Fashion.'

'The Parke', Morning Post[17]

Of course there were other ways to get around in the Regency world, but moving from place to place sometimes came secondary to being seen doing so, and not every outing required a vehicle. Promenading was an invaluable chance to throw on your most fashionable walking gear and stroll out among society. One didn't necessarily walk to get anywhere – why else would one's illustrious family employ coachmen? – but simply, as with so many other things in the Regency, to observe society.

Riding side-saddle was much harder than sitting astride, but it was the more elegant style of horse riding expected of women of the ton. Another opportunity to be seen in the right place at the right time, taking a ride in Hyde Park was a chance to dress up in military-inspired riding gear and join the gossiping circles of the ton.

*Bridgerton* fans cannot fail to have noticed the importance of promenading for their heroes and heroines. While taking a stroll through town or picturesque parkland could be a hobby in itself, it was also a chance to see and be seen by one's would-be suitors and the tastemakers of the ton. When Daphne and the Duke of Hastings promenaded together in public, it was a statement that could and would not go unnoticed. Just as they had planned, it left everyone with the impression that Daphne was to be considered a catch, since a duke had shown an interest in her. It also suggested to ambitious mothers and social-climbing debutantes that the Duke of Hastings was no longer on the market.

Yet a promenade could backfire too. After Edwina and Anthony's marriage plans fell apart so disastrously, they were the talk of the town, and when their families went out to promenade in an effort to show a brave face, they found themselves shunned by the ton.

Likewise, riding on Hyde Park's Rotten Row was an unmissable opportunity to make an impression, whether you were a gent in his most well-fitting buckskin breeches or a lady in a fashionably cut riding habit, taking its cues from the military coats of the men who had conquered Napoleon. While horses were transportation for some, for others horse riding was a social stage and a chance to cut a dash and really show off. For *Bridgerton*'s fans, horse riding also provided them with some of the most dramatic moments of the show. Fans will remember that Kate and Anthony met in the saddle, then risked scandal when they stole away together during a hunt for a smouldering lesson in marksmanship.

Climbing into the saddle was as much a pastime as a necessity. Like so many other things in the world of the ton, it was tied up with wealth and fashion and was an opportunity for gentlemen to look suitably manly or for ladies to look suitably accomplished, whether maintaining their graceful poise in the saddle or driving a picturesque gig. Carriages needed horses to pull them, but carriage horses weren't always the best choice for riding, and of course mounting the right horse was just as important as wearing the right boots or dancing at the right venue. In the world of the ton, everything was about making an impression, and that included the horses in the stable too.

'Hyde Park on a Sunday'. London's parks offered the perfect expanses for promenading and horse riding, and another chance to show off the family wealth and planned romantic engagements to the rest of the ton.

For families who were lucky enough to have a carriage *and* riding horses, there was no possibility that they'd be seen giving room in the paddock to just any old nag. While horses could be rented, this was far from the purview of the wealthy, and they valued a stable filled with fine equines just as some covet a garage full of expensive cars today. From the matched ponies that would pull a lady's gig when she took the air, to the fine hunters and trotters available for a ride through the estates of the wealthy, the array of mounts was bewildering to those who didn't know their horseflesh. But of course, *le bon ton* knew it to a tee.

Once the stables were stocked with the best on offer, it was time to take to the saddle – and which type depended on your gender. Men rode astride while ladies were expected to master side-saddle, the only way to travel for the sake of propriety. Riding side-saddle competently takes considerably more skill than riding astride, but since ladies began to learn the skill in childhood, by the time they were out in public it was supposedly second nature to them. Graceful and poised atop her mount, a young lady would have made sure any potential suitors got a very good look at her as she rode out in the sunshine.

Each afternoon the wealthy came to Hyde Park's Rotten Row to ride their finest horses, while carriages were driven on South Carriage Drive, and these daily gatherings offered observers a chance to glimpse the rich and famous at play. When it came to getting attention in the world of the ton, it was a question of using everything you had, from dance floors to side-saddle and anything in between.

# CHAPTER FOUR

# SOCIAL OCCASIONS

'People continue to be gay both in town and country spite
of the hot weather, race meetings and the approaching
sporting season. The halls of the nobility ... still extend
their profuse hospitalities and congregate together
the leaders of the ton: but to distinguish each of the
splendid parties, balls, fêtes &c., &c. is quite impossible
in the compass of our present pages; let it suffice that
taste and art were exhausted to supply the profusion.'

'Parties, Balls, Routs, &c., &c.', *The World of
Fashion and Continental Feuilletons*[18]

ridgertonians will already be familiar with the
Season, the glamorous, sometimes cut-throat world
of fashionable London over which the members of
the ton reigned. Once a year, as Parliament was in session
between January and June, the most glittering members of

the upper classes – and those who hoped to join them – left their opulent country estates and travelled to their equally luxurious homes in the capital. There, they played out their lives for all to see and envy, and getting an invitation to the right event or the most impressive home could be an invaluable badge of social honour; it was a real sign that you'd made it. Vast sums of money were lavished on everything from dress to food to entertainment, and all with one aim: to be seen at the absolute top of the ton.

An etching by Regency artist and caricaturist Thomas Rowlandson. Here, a soldier bows to a young woman as her social set look on and card players while away the evening in the background.

# THE SEASON

The Season served a number of purposes, but two were chief among them. Firstly, it gave the upper classes something to do while Parliament was sitting. Since members of both the Commons and the Lords were all in town and looking not only to move and shake but to keep their families out of their hair, the Season provided just the distraction they needed. And of course, it was a networking opportunity par excellence, whether for business, politics or even romance. This segues neatly into its second function, and the one for which it is perhaps most famous: the Season became vital in the dynasty-building of the elite, as it offered unmarried members of the upper classes – and their ambitious parents – ample opportunity to peruse the matches on offer. It was a chance to perhaps make some lasting connections and hopefully snag a spouse.

During the Season, families took turns to host events themselves and attend those hosted by others. While some might be in public spaces such as assembly rooms, others were held in the eye-wateringly opulent homes of the rich and influential. The residences in which the ton entertained were elegant, richly appointed and run by a well-drilled team of domestic servants overseen by the lady of the house. The ton's townhouse typically began with a basement below street level, topped by three or four storeys where the family and their servants lived. While the sitting room and dining room would be on the ground floor, the most esteemed visitors were allowed to visit the first-floor drawing room, usually the finest in the whole house. This was the place where the householders could really show off, at least in that unostentatious way that was so important to Regency tastemakers. To be seen to flaunt one's privilege in anything but the most casual, understated manner was a definite no-no ... unless one was the Prince Regent.

Socializing in the Regency was a serious business, and it could take all day. While members of royalty had traditionally dined in public so their subjects could catch a glimpse of them, such a thing was certainly not par for the course for members of the ton. In general, mornings were spent privately, with gentlemen attending to their business and ladies to their correspondence. Once these duties were out of the way, it was time for morning visits.

Armed with their visiting cards in case the people they were hoping to see weren't at home, the fashionable set out on their round of calls. This early socializing was a chance to catch up on the news that might have been missed or to share the latest gossip. The visits could be formal or casual, depending on who was making them, and they were a vital part of the morning routine. Taken over light refreshments, these calls were the first outings in a packed day of being noticed.

A lady's afternoon might be spent browsing fashionable shops or taking a promenade or ride while gents were attending to business or perhaps sitting in Parliament. All of this, of course, was a precursor to the evening, which was when things really promised to come alive. *Bridgerton*'s world turns on balls and social gatherings, and the real life of the Regency was certainly little different. From balls to routs to opulent dinners rich with intrigue, there was always something happening to entertain the ton.

# JOIN THE CLUB

**'[The] requisites for a Statesman were few and insignificant indeed; that it was the only business which needed no apprenticeship, no study, no training; that it was enough to belong to Brooks's or White's, and to make fine speeches in Parliament.'**

'The Political Examiner', *The Examiner*[19]

In a world where making an impression was part of the game, being seen in the right place was everything. For gentlemen, one's politics dictated one's club and whether you would be hitting the gambling tables in Brooks's on Pall Mall or in White's on St James's Street. It was possible to do both, but few men had the connections to pull that off. White's is the oldest club in London and is still only open to men today. It first opened its doors in 1693 and was soon the most exclusive address in town, eventually becoming the unofficial headquarters of the governing Tories in the Georgian era.

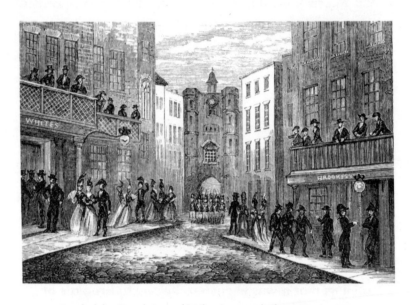

Rival clubs Brooks's and White's provided private meeting grounds for political whisperings – and more importantly, they offered the ton's menfolk an exclusive space for drinking and gambling away from prying female eyes.

Beau Brummell could often be glimpsed holding court at White's, where he had his own table in front of an elegant picture window where he entertained friends including the ballooning Prince Regent. Membership of White's was difficult to achieve for any but those of the aristocratic class, and before a man could be admitted the existing members were polled by placing either a black or a white ball into a bag.

A white ball meant a vote in favour, while black meant a vote against, and one single black ball was enough to destroy the chances of an ambitious would-be member.

In 1762, two blackballed gentlemen who had been denied membership of White's set up a meeting society, laying the foundations for a competing club that would one day become Brooks's. This competing club opened its doors in 1764 with the support of over two dozen illustrious Whig nobles, meeting in a building owned by William Almack. The club moved into a purpose-built clubhouse a few years later thanks to financing by William Brooks, the moneylender who presided over it and in whose honour it was named.

Just as White's became the unofficial Tory HQ, Brooks's soon established itself as the unofficial meeting place of the Whig opposition, but it was as famous for its gambling rooms as for its members. Fortunes were won and lost in the blink of an eye, and men staked everything on the most bizarre wagers they or anybody else could imagine.

Brooks's and White's shared their members with other, smaller clubs, such as Watier's, which was opened to showcase the skills of the Prince Regent's personal chef, Jean-Baptiste Watier. Watier fed his employer's immense appetite and the elite members of the club, while on the gaming tables 'at Watier's Club both princes and nobles lost or gained fortunes between themselves'.[20] Every club, whether small or large, existed to feed the insatiable appetite for gambling among the denizens of the Regency. Everyone gambled, from high-rollers placing bets on which raindrop might reach the bottom of a window first, to polite middle-class wives at card parties and beyond. All that was required was to gamble in a controlled manner, rather than letting one's debts get out of hand. Many failed to heed that rule.

The result of the founding members being 'blackballed' from their attempt to join White's, Brooks's was home to the opposition Whig Party – and the site of riches made and lost on its infamous gambling tables.

While the clubs offered gentlemen a male-only environment in which to loosen their cravats, they also hosted exclusive events that were open to both men and women. Balls were given to celebrate notable occasions, but only the wealthiest could hope to attend, and these were among the highlights of the Season.

# MAKING IT AT ALMACK'S

In a city bristling with impressive and exclusive venues, one towered above them all. Almack's Assembly Rooms on King Street was the golden ticket for the ton. It emerged from the same confusion of clubs that spawned Brooks's and rose swiftly to the very top of the tree. For Bridgertonians, receiving a coveted voucher for Almack's would be like reserving a place in heaven.

Almack's started life many years before the Regency as a Curzon Street coffee house owned by William Almack. There was nothing particularly notable about the place, but it enjoyed steady business from its opening in 1754 until 1762, when a society was formed that became the very first private club to be associated with William Almack. The society grew and clubs sprouted from it like leaves from a tree, growing in wealth, prestige and importance with every new development.

Mr Almack the coffee house keeper amassed a fortune and proved to have an eye for what fashionable Georgians wanted. He opened Almack's Assembly Rooms in 1765, providing a place in which men and women could pay a subscription to socialize in the most exclusive manner imaginable. By the time of the Regency, Almack's had become the most fashionable address in Regency London, and though William Almack himself didn't live to see it, his name has become forever associated with the peak of *Bridgerton*-esque glamour.

An evening at Almack's. A voucher to the assembly rooms was a golden ticket, promising connections with the great and the good of fashionable society on an epic dance floor. The food, however, left something to be desired.

Just as gentlemen hoping to join an exclusive club had to be proposed, vouched for and voted upon, so too did prospective Almack's members face a fearsome selection. The committee who decided the membership of Almack's was made of a changing panel of Lady Patronesses, and the primary aim of every ambitious society mother was to see her daughter selected to receive a voucher that would grant admittance to the fabled venue. The most influential patronesses during the reign of the Prince Regent were Amelia Stewart, Viscountess

Castlereagh; Sarah Villiers, Countess of Jersey; Emily Clavering-Cowper, Countess Cowper; Maria Molyneux, Countess of Sefton; the Honourable Sarah Clementina Drummond-Burrell; Dorothea Lieven, Countess de Lieven; and Maria Theresia, Countess Esterházy. Each year hundreds of requests for vouchers rolled in and the patronesses sifted through them, making and smashing dreams with a word.

*They can open or shut the doors of fashionable life on them, by the mere circumstance of giving or withholding a ticket to Almack's – the proudest and most aristocratic family in the land are fain to bow down, and with cap in hand, to use a homely but expressive phrase, supplicate 'a subscription' from this 'coalition cabal'.[21]*

Though we might expect wealth to be one sure-fire way of gaining admittance, that wasn't necessarily the case. In fact, being considered nouveau riche was one of the worst offences that could be committed in the eyes of the ton, and breeding went far further than bank balance. A noble title was certainly a desirable trait for would-be dancers at Almack's, and fitting into the ideal standards of behaviour was equally valuable – but most important of all was that none of the patronesses had any reason to dislike an applicant. After all, even the notorious Lady Caroline Lamb was kicked out of Almack's when she satirized Lady Jersey in her novel *Glenarvon*.

Rumour and gossip abounded in the ton, and even the wealthiest and most famous weren't exempt – including the Duke of Wellington. Chatter had it that Napoleon's vanquisher was turned away by Almack's patronesses, a medal or two being no excuse for poor timekeeping.

The Lady Patronesses of Almack's each had their own method of dealing with the avalanche of membership requests, from the kindly Lady Sefton's gentle manner to the brash Lady Jersey, nicknamed 'Silence' due to her loud-mouthed rudeness, and nobody was beyond their reach. Sometimes they would accept the voucher request of a wife but reject her spouse, no doubt ruffling a few feathers at home, and even the biggest names in Great Britain were subject to their scrutiny. When the Duke of Wellington arrived at Almack's wearing trousers rather than obeying the dress code that specified men must be clad in dark knee breeches and silk stockings, a dark coat and a white cravat, he was politely turned away due to his attire. Or so rumour had it. Another version of the story claimed that Lady Jersey turned Wellington away because he had reached Almack's just seven minutes after the doors were locked to new arrivals. Whatever the truth, if the Iron Duke could be turned away, nobody was safe.

Each Wednesday night a grand ball was held at Almack's, and you'd be forgiven for picturing it as the peak of opulence in every sense. In many ways it was, but some elements might well surprise you. A small orchestra led the dancing on a floor that measured 100ft x 40ft, with dancers gliding between classical columns, illuminated by lights that flickered from ornate cut-glass sconces. The light was reflected by vast mirrors, through which each corner of the dance floor could be observed by the Lady Patronesses, who sat on a dais graciously acknowledging each arrival. So far, so glam, but if the surroundings were extravagant, refreshment was anything but.

Attendees at Almack's were offered a choice of weak lemonade, orgeat (a sweet drink of almonds) or ratafia (water infused with a sweet concoction of spices or fruits). Food, meanwhile, was limited to dry cake and exceptionally thin slices of day-old buttered bread. No alcohol was served, so while the ladies were sober, plenty of men rolled up once they'd been sure to get themselves thoroughly lubricated. The only rule was that they had to be sure to turn up before 11 p.m., when the doors were locked and no further visitors were admitted to join the ball, which would go on into the early hours of the next morning.

Ticketing was open to those who had successfully applied for one of the coveted Almack's vouchers, which cost 10 guineas per year, approximately £400 today. Voucher holders were allowed to purchase a ticket for themselves at a cost of 10 shillings, approximately £20, and to propose a plus-one, who either gained permission to attend on a 'strangers ticket' or received the dreaded black ball of rejection.

Getting into Almack's opened virtually every other door like magic, but with hundreds of applicants for every voucher, it was inevitable that some hopeful candidates would be disappointed. Rejection could be temporary or permanent, but the candidate would never know if there was any point reapplying next Season. Nor would they know why they had been rejected, since they would learn of the decision only via a form circular that the applicant had to call to receive. For rejects, there were other, smaller balls at which they could content themselves as they reflected on the fact that while they may not have cracked the big time this Season, nor had they seen it entirely snatched away from them. There was always next year, after all, if the Lady Patronesses decreed it.

Although not receiving an Almack's voucher was

disappointing, to have one and then lose it was a catastrophe. Every Monday night during the Season, the Lady Patronesses assembled to review the list of voucher-holders and remove those who they felt no longer deserved the honour. This was far worse than never making the cut in the first place, and among the ton it was like having one's head cut off.

Of course, Almack's wasn't the only place to dance. Private balls given by grand families could cost a fortune to put on, offering dancing and an impressive feast far removed from the meagre repast on offer at the premier assembly rooms. In fact, refreshments at private parties offered another opportunity for networking and showing off, with grand Sunday dinners providing a chance for the high and mighty to get some politicking done alongside their socializing.

For a more frivolous entertainment, some members of the upper classes liked to put on their own theatricals at home, as readers of *Mansfield Park* will attest. Musical gatherings such as those enjoyed by the King and Queen in the early years of their marriage were another popular way to entertain more intimate friends. If one really wanted to make a splash, then why not hire in the biggest names in showbiz and have them perform for your guests at an exclusive soirée? It certainly beat charades.

# A GAD ABOUT
# THE PLEASURE GARDENS

'Says I to Doll, the other day,
We've lately not much fun done,
And so suppose we take the coach,
And journey up to London.
Why, yes, says Doll, I do not care,
I'll go if you are willing,
And we'll see all the Vauxhall sights,
For they only charge a shilling.'

'Vauxhall for One Shilling'[22]

When one fancied something a little less exclusive than Almack's and a little more glitzy than a night at home, the pleasure gardens at Vauxhall offered the perfect solution.

About a mile from the centre of the city, Vauxhall Pleasure Gardens was one of the most spectacular sights in England, and for 3 shillings visitors could enjoy its wonders for the night. The gardens were laid out as a series of tree-lined avenues illuminated by more than 20,000 lights, and they offered a magical world in which everything was decorated and dressed to perfection. Fashionable visitors strolled through the enchanted lanes before taking their

A night at Vauxhall was the perfect opportunity to promenade with a beau while taking in the beautiful scenery, made magical with over 20,000 lights, glittering mechanized waterworks and epic firework displays.

seats in a newly constructed Grecian temple to enjoy an orchestral concert, or took supper within the breathtaking rotunda, surrounded by works of art by the most celebrated painters of the day. Vauxhall was particularly famed for its dazzling mechanized waterworks, where elaborate displays showed off a watermill and fountains, demonstrating the height of Regency modernity. Once the ton had been thoroughly entertained, a magnificent firework display brought the evening to a close and sent visitors home to their townhouses to rest before starting another round of visits and intrigue tomorrow.

Entertainment in the Regency was plentiful, whether it was offered by the celebrated circus at Astley's Amphitheatre or the menagerie of exotic beasts at the Tower of London. Of course, visiting the theatre was popular among all social classes, and with the Regent having something of a penchant for actresses, he was a regular sight at the Opera House or in one of the royal boxes. One couldn't be said to have *done* London theatre if one hadn't watched the great Shakespearian Edmund Kean emote as nobody had ever emoted before or heard Angelica Catalani sing an aria.

Yet the Regent didn't always attend the theatre to watch what was on stage. Sometimes he went there to show off his latest noble mistress or to pick out another leading lady to join his conquests. Indeed, on one occasion his mother even asked one of his actress mistresses to be removed from the opposite box when she went to see a play; the mistress refused to go. However, as the majority of the Regent's mistresses discovered, her reign was to be a short one. Once the outspoken actress' lustre dimmed and her lover had moved onto his next fancy, there was no seat in Prinny's box for the woman who had dared to say no to Queen Charlotte. Life as the mistress of the Prince Regent was filled with glamour and excitement, but it was only ever a temporary engagement.

# THE CARLTON HOUSE FÊTE

The Prince Regent's Carlton House, though ultimately demolished in 1826, for a time played host to the most opulent and exclusive Regency parties. The most famous of these was ostensibly held in the King's name but really offered an excuse for the Regent to gift himself a 4,000-piece silver-gilt dining set.

It seems only right that we end our jaunt through the social life of the Regency with the event that might be said to have started it: the Carlton House Fête. Never one to miss an opportunity to hold a massive party, when the Prince of Wales was appointed Regent he decided to celebrate the occasion in fine style. There was just one problem: Prinny had only come to power because of his father's catastrophic mental decline. If he partied now, while the King was in crisis, it would look like the height of bad taste. What he needed was a plan; luckily, he was a born schemer.

Years earlier, Queen Charlotte had celebrated her husband's birthday with elaborate entertainments in the gardens of her Buckingham Palace home. There were shadow plays and ornamental gardens and everything to delight the eye and ear, but over the decades these entertainments had become more than she or the ailing monarch could bear. Now the King's June birthday was marked by a stuffy drawing room, but that wasn't the Prince Regent's style.

He conceived of a grand fête at his opulent Carlton House home, not to honour *him* but to mark the birthday of his illustrious father. The invitations became the most coveted ticket in the land and the guest list was managed by Lady Hertford, the Regent's current mistress. When one anonymous peer's wife, known only as *Lady W*, didn't receive an invitation, diarist Joseph Farington mischievously speculated that perhaps the paper invitations had run out by the time they reached the letter 'W'. 'That could not be,' was her reply, 'for half the W[hore]s in town were invited.' The guests of honour were members of the exiled French royal family, but notably missing from the eventual attendees was Queen Charlotte. She refused to join the event to demonstrate both her support for her husband and her disapproval of her sons. Unsurprisingly, she kept her adult daughters away too.

*The history of our amusements presents no species of spectacle such as we are now about to describe: it was a chef-d'oeuvre which, in splendour and variety, never, we believe, was equalled in any age or country.*[23]

Some 2,000 of the most important names in society would eventually be invited to the party on 19 June 1811, and it seemed as though every tradesman, artisan and fashionable firm in London was called upon to play a part. In addition to magnificent entertainments and the feast to end all feasts, the already over-the-top environment of Carlton House was to be transformed into a temple of pleasure and excess. There would be pavilions and immense floral displays, glittering sideshows and delightful little treats for those who cared to wander in the gardens. Enormous dining tents and a bandstand to house the orchestra were erected, while the entire perimeter of the mansion was closed off to prevent gatecrashers. Even the guy ropes that held up the tents were gilded, while beautiful lanterns hidden in the trees turned the grounds into an enchanted playground. Inside the house the opulence continued, and nobody could miss the elaborate chalk art that had been applied to the polished floors of the grand ballroom.

*In the centre appears G. III R. with the*
*Royal Crown and supporters; the whole*
*encircled, in a highly emblazoned manner, by*
*the rose, the thistle, and the shamrock.*[24]

Chalk art like this was a sign of true wealth. It was expensive, beautiful and utterly temporary, soon lost forever beneath the dancing feet that blurred it into oblivion.

It took some real chutzpah to stand out in an ocean of the most expensive gowns and finest jewellery the ton could muster, but the Prince Regent managed it. He dressed in the scarlet uniform of a field marshal, a rank he had awarded himself just a short time before, and strode like a peacock through the crowds, who took three hours to file through the gates. Jewels glittered out from the Regent's corpulent corseted figure, and upon his head he wore a curled, heavy wig, set off by a pair of bushy fake sideburns.

The Regent was seated at the head of the state banquet table in the gothic conservatory, and he basked at the centre of the stage. Everything about the prince's table, which he shared with hundreds of the most honoured guests, was beyond extra. A marble channel of water ran down the centre of the table through which live fish swam, while the fountain that supplied it ran down into a small lake, around which miniatures of classical ruins had been erected. This was no casual gathering but a circus, and the Regent presided over it all as ringmaster. He was framed by the Grand Service, which glittered out from its bed of crimson silk.

*The excellence of design and exquisiteness of*
*workmanship could not be exceeded; it exhibited*
*a grandeur beyond description; while the many*
*and various purposes for which gold and silver*
*materials were used were equally beautiful*
*and superb in all their minute details.*[25]

The Grand Service was a silver-gilt dining service of over 4,000 pieces, made by Rundell, Bridge & Rundell, the royal goldsmiths. The magnificent set dazzled everyone who saw it, and the Regent made sure nobody could miss it, or him. Those who sat at his table in the gothic conservatory were the most honoured of all guests, and when they were served from the Grand Service, everybody knew it.

The fête at Carlton House was ostensibly to celebrate the birthday of George III, and it was only right that the most generous gift of all was sent by his son, the Prince Regent. The only problem was, he sent it to himself. Prinny gifted himself the Grand Service, the epitome of his collection of precious and priceless metals.

The country had never seen a show like the one that unfolded at Carlton House that night. By the time the doors opened at 9 p.m. there were guests lined up into the distance, all of them resplendent in their finest uniforms, suits or gowns. In the sultry summer evening they dined and danced and revelled in the fact that they were among the chosen few – or 2,000 – who had been called upon to witness this once-in-a-lifetime evening. Dinner was served at 2 a.m. before fireworks burst into colourful blossoms in the skies over Carlton House. By the time the party finally broke up, dawn had long since broken.

Not everyone was impressed. Percy Bysshe Shelley wrote, 'It is said that this entertainment will cost £120,000. Nor will it be the last bauble which the nation must buy to amuse this overgrown bantling of Regency.'[26] He was proven right too, for though the fête initially improved the Regent's standing with the public, before long it had plummeted lower than ever, with critics daubing 'Bread or the Regent's Head' on the walls of Carlton House. However, Prinny carried on regardless, never learning a lesson simply because he didn't believe he needed to.

In the world of the ton, ostentatious displays of wealth were to be frowned upon and everything must be done in the best taste. When it came to the Prince Regent, however, that rule was overturned by one very simple fact: *he* was the star of the show, whatever the politicians and public tried to tell him.

# CHAPTER FIVE

# THE MEDIA

'The freedom of the press is the bulwark of British liberty; but the public gazettes should discuss public affairs, and not become the vehicle of private scandal.'

James Lawrence, *The Empire of the Nairs*[27]

In the world of *Bridgerton*, one person alone seems to know all the juiciest gossip that the ton would love to keep under their immaculately millinered hats. The mysterious Lady Whistledown is the woman in the know, and her *dearest readers* can't get enough of it. In her unmissable genteel pamphlet, *Lady Whistledown's Society Papers*, she shares scandals, secrets and scurrilous gossip.

Lady Whistledown's true identity was kept a closely guarded secret until it was sensationally revealed – no spoilers here – and audiences have become hooked on her stories, just as the Bridgertons and their social circle did back in the days of the

Regency. She is, of course, a fictional character of Julia Quinn's creation, but there are precedents for Lady Whistledown in the proto-gossip columns of the Georgian and Regency eras.

Mrs Phoebe Crackenthorpe, 'a Lady that knows everything', was as close as the long eighteenth century got to its very own Lady Whistledown, even though she predated the world of *Bridgerton* by a good century. Mrs Crackenthorpe was the anonymous author behind *The Female Tatler*, which was a magazine published between 1709 and 1710. *The Female Tatler* was aimed at a female audience and satirized the personalities and stories of the day, with a good dose of gossip besides. Though her writing career was short-lived, Mrs Crackenthorpe is arguably Lady Whistledown's spiritual grandmother, and unlike Lady W her identity remains a mystery to this very day.

# WHAT TO READ

During the Regency gossip was currency, and everyone from polite ladies making their morning visits to the patrons of clubs and coffee houses loved to discuss the news and personalities of the day. If they needed a prompt, they could find plenty to chew over in the latest edition of *Town and Country Magazine*, which hosted the unmissable 'Tête-à-Tête' column. Scandal sheets were not known in the Regency, but 'Tête-à-Tête' was as close as it got. Each column spotlighted a particularly notorious couple and reported on their comings and goings, keeping their names redacted and their images in silhouette. Guessing the identities of these silhouettes was almost as much fun as reading about their antics, and they were the equivalent of modern blind gossip features on the internet, which stay on the right side of the law while ensuring speculation gets as fevered as possible.

Staying on the right side of the law seemed like the easiest thing in the world to the journalists and gossip-mongers of the Regency. When they wrote about the Prince of Wales romancing actress Mary Robinson, the couple became known in the press as Florizel and Perdita, after the lovers in *The Winter's Tale*. Mary was appearing in the play when they met, and they referred to themselves as the fictional paramours in the love notes they exchanged. When there was no obvious nickname to call upon, the press simply ladled on the hints, so rumours about arguments involving *an illustrious lady* in the royal box would clearly refer to Caroline of Brunswick, Prinny's estranged wife. Sometimes they weren't even as subtle as that, and stories of the D— of Y— employed a code so simple that everybody knew they were reading about the Regent's favourite brother.

For those who wanted more than simple gossip and scandal, there were other options available. Between 1770 and 1818 *The Lady's Magazine, or Entertaining Companion for the Fair Sex* offered female readers a very popular diversion. Though it largely avoided politics, the magazine touched on news and current affairs, fiction, culture, fashion and society gossip. Its needlework patterns were particularly popular, and it prided itself on being of appeal to a broad social church. Those who wanted to believe that their choice of gossip was a little more salubrious than that of the newspapers turned to the popular *Fashionable World* column, or even to the less widespread *Fashionable Faux Pas*, which offered a rundown of not just who was partnering who to fashionable balls and events but what they were wearing and how brightly their jewels glittered. Not for *The Lady's Magazine* or *Fashionable World* stories of Caroline of Brunswick with her hand down her chamberlain's breeches on a road trip through Italy. For that, one would have to buy a *respectable* newspaper.

Of course, newspapers didn't only spread gossip. The Whig and Tory press took turns to throw mud at their opponents, while radical publications agitated for direct action in the face of rising poverty, hunger and the Regent's extravagant ways. When the marriage of the Prince Regent and his wife ended in spectacular style the press divided into pro-prince and pro-princess, with the former reporting breathless stories of Caroline's moral turpitude on the Continent while the latter painted her as a broken-hearted, ill-used wife. There really is nothing new about the press wars and bias of the modern era, other than the fact that the eighteenth-century gentlemen of the press had an eye for savagery that would send even the hungriest modern shark scurrying for cover. Not everyone got away with it, though; just ask Leigh Hunt, who received a prison sentence for libel after he dismissed the Prince Regent as 'a violator of his word, a libertine over head and ears in debt and disgrace, a despiser of domestic ties, the companion of gamblers, and demireps, a man who has just closed half a century without one single claim on the gratitude of his country or the respect of posterity!'[28]

Caroline of Brunswick, like the most famous celebrities today, was perfect fodder for the tabloids of her era, gladly feeding gossip and scandal wherever she went.

The only true way to get right to the heart of the juiciest gossip of all was to look at the legal papers that detailed the in-depth business of criminal conversation cases. These were, essentially, adultery cases, and nobody was above them. Even the King's own brother had found his sex life detailed in a crim. con. suit, which caused a shuddering rift in the eighteenth-century royal family. Obviously not everybody had the means to access these papers, but gossip spread like wildfire once it was started, and no secret seemed truly safe from the ears of the public.

# CARICATURES AND COURTESANS

In a world where literacy was far from universal, news and gossip spread not only in print but in pictures and orally too. From genteel ladies undertaking their daily visits, to the raucous clubhouses where gentlemen gathered, gossip wasn't only something to titillate but to use as leverage that could influence all manner of things. Printshop windows were filled with merciless caricatures that poked fun at everything from the Regent's corpulent bottom to scrawny actresses who enchanted audiences and tempted peers. Spending some time browsing the windows of printmakers was like browsing a favourite Instagram feed, where visuals could tell a story in a matter of seconds.

Artists like James Gillray and Thomas Rowlandson made their reputations with their savage, satirical, lewd and often hilarious caricatures. Nobody was off-limits, no subject too delicate for their pens, and the likes of Hannah Humphrey's printshop became destinations in themselves, with heaving throngs gathered to see what was hanging in the window.

Not to be outdone, newspapers made up for their lack of illustrations with breathless descriptions of the participants in a scandal. When the Duke of York was under investigation by the House of Lords for his alleged participation in a cash-for-military-promotion scandal operated by his mistress, courtesan Mary Anne Clarke, she was the undoubted star of the show. Newspapers fell over themselves to publish intricate descriptions of her 'light blue silk gown and coat' and her 'fair, clear, smooth skin, and lively blue eyes',[29] while printshop windows filled up with illustrations showing the unrepentant courtesan and the prince who should have known better.

And then, of course, there were the memoirs. In a world where courtesans knew the secrets of the high and mighty better than anyone, some of them wielded almost unthinkable power. Perhaps the most infamous was Harriette Wilson, who had been a courtesan since her adolescence, when 'I shall not say why

and how I became, at the age of fifteen, the mistress of the Earl of Craven'. Her career was long and illustrious, but when she grew older and her patrons abandoned her for younger women, Harriette was left high and dry. The nobles she had served had promised to take care of her in her mature years, but to a man they let her down.

Abandoned by her once loyal patrons, courtesan Harriette Wilson used one of the only tools available to her as a woman: the pen. Offering the men who had deserted her the opportunity to remove their names from her scandalous memoirs for a fee, she became rich from the project. 'Publish, and be damned,' said the Duke of Wellington.

In reply, Harriette began to write her serialized memoirs, which promised to pull back the bedsheets on the most famous men in the country. Before each weekly instalment was published Harriette wrote to the men who would feature and asked them for £200 to remove their names from the manuscript. Many handed over the cash, but the Duke of Wellington would do no such thing. He famously told Harriette to 'publish, and be damned', and she did just that. The conquering hero of popular myth was nothing to write home about for Miss Wilson, who dismissed him as 'very like a rat-catcher', a bore in bed and a curmudgeon out of it. So much for the Iron Duke!

# CHAPTER SIX

# HEALTH AND HYGIENE

**'People are told, that if they dip the least into medical knowledge, it will render them fanciful, and make them believe they have got every disease of which they read. This I am satisfied will seldom be the case with sensible people.'**

William Buchan, *Domestic Medicine, or A Treatise on the Prevention and Cure of Diseases by Regimen and Simple Medicines*[30]

n the Regency, medicine was in a state of change. With home remedies long practised by people who usually had no formal training, the landscape had begun to shift with the opening of medical schools, to which gentlemen flocked eager to gain the title of physician and the honorarium that would come with it. In a world in which tinctures, potions and cure-alls were sold on what seemed like every street corner, health was often in the purview of the domestic sphere. Of course, members of the ton would have had access to the best and most illustrious physicians money could buy, but for general matters of health and hygiene there might not be any need to call in a professional at all.

# MIASMAS AND PASSIONS

During the long eighteenth century, it was popularly believed that the cause of illness was something called 'miasmas', namely bad air. The idea of dangerous miasmas originated with Galen, who also put forward the theory of the four humors, which posited that there were four elements that made up the human body: earth, which was associated with black bile; air, which was associated with blood; water, associated with phlegm; and fire, associated with yellow bile. To ensure good health, one had to maintain a good balance of the humors, and should they get out of balance thanks to any number of causes ranging from emotion and anxiety to miasmas and fluctuating temperatures, then illness would doubtlessly ensue.

Every home would have contained a copy of at least one medical manual, and one of the most popular was physician William Buchan's *Domestic Medicine, or A Treatise on the*

*Prevention and Cure of Diseases by Regimen and Simple Medicines: With Observations on Sea-bathing, and the Use of the Mineral Waters, to Which Is Annexed, a Dispensatory for the Use of Private Practitioners.* The book was already half a century old when the Regency began, but it was considered the last word on the matter of health and hygiene, and it strongly advocated for the theory of the four humors. Everything from sleeping with the window open to allowing a young lady to get too excited could bring on a fever, and a fever could be deadly, so steadiness was the order of the day for the women of the ton.

> *When hysteric fits are occasioned by sympathy, they may be cured by exciting an opposite passion. This is said to have been the case of a whole school of young ladies in Holland, who were all cured by being told that the first who was seized should be burnt to death … I have known madness itself brought on by sympathy.*[31]

Violent emotions were to be avoided at all costs, lest the likes of Dr Francis Willis, who had straitjacketed, gagged and blistered George III, be called in to administer leeches and drain out blood in the hope that it would cure the patient. Pity the poor Regency denizen who had no choice but to submit to surgery with no anaesthetic to dull the senses. Frances Burney underwent a successful mastectomy in 1811 under the supervision of celebrated battlefield surgeon Baron

Dominique-Jean Larrey. Her writings on the operation and 'the glitter of polished steel', as she wrote to her sister, are chilling in an age of anaesthetic and ever-expanding medical technologies.

'Opening a Vein' by Thomas Rowlandson. In efforts to 'balance the humors', draining patients of blood was a common practice in the Regency era and was believed to rid the body of impure fluids.

Some of the most common treatments of the Regency make us squirm today, and none more so than the use of leeches for bloodletting. One man who certainly paid the price for bloodletting was the notorious Lord Byron, whose doctors prescribed a course of bleeding when he fell ill early in 1824. Instead of curing the poet, the treatment only left him weaker than ever – yet Byron's physicians continued to bleed him to relieve his ongoing symptoms. He died that April of a fever, having been fatally weakened by bloodletting.

This method was a go-to for physicians looking to treat a huge variety of ailments, and it could be done in two ways. One was to apply leeches to the patient, something the King was no stranger to, and the other was to make a cut out of which blood could be syphoned. By removing what was thought to be excess blood from the body, it was believed that most illnesses could be cured or at least alleviated.

# DO IT YOURSELF

Ever alert to the dangers facing them, the households of the ton would all have kept their own ornate medicine chests for less serious complaints. Though they would likely have contained some pre-mixed preparations, DIY home remedies were common at all levels of society, and a well-stocked garden could provide a lady or her maid with all manner of herbs, spices and plants for use in tinctures and potions. This knowledge had been passed down the generations not by learned medical men but by the women who had kept house and absorbed all they knew from their own mothers and grandmothers before them. Long before medicine was licensed and pharmaceutical companies churned out potions and pills, the women of the world were mixing their own, and some of them might raise eyebrows today. After all, it's rare indeed that we would find opium in a bathroom cabinet, but in the Regency it was an essential ingredient in home medicine. Laudanum, meanwhile, was a cure-all that eventually became one of the ailing Regent's favourite and most destructive vices.

If all else failed, a trip to take the waters at somewhere like Bath or Cheltenham might revive the spirits, while many people, including the royal family, favoured a seaside cure. In these cases families would travel to fashionable resorts such as Brighton and Weymouth and spend a summer away from the city, taking the sea air. 'The happy effects of the sea cure are most clear and indisputable,' wrote one author, celebrating the sea's powers when it came to 'a large number of troubles, rickets, scrofula, tuberculosis, especially local tubercular disease, such as white swellings, hip-joint disease, and Pott's disease'.[32] George III's daughter, Princess Amelia, spent long hours undertaking a seaside cure for the ailments that eventually led to her early death, so we can surmise that it certainly wasn't a faultless solution.

When it came to domestic hygiene, some people's standards were higher than others. The Prince Regent was fastidious in his toilette, and rumours of his estranged wife's lack of hygiene were encouraged by the prince and his supporters. Caroline of Brunswick made a virtue of deliberately rushing through her toilette, and on her wedding night she disgusted her husband with 'such marks of filth both in the fore and hind part of her ... that she turned my stomach and from that moment I made a vow never to touch her again'. The prince was far from an impartial judge, but independent witnesses agreed that Caroline of Brunswick's hygiene left something to be desired.

To the movers and shakers of the ton, such a thought was too dreadful to imagine, and good hygiene was vital. Just like carriages, fashion and holidays, one's cleanliness regime offered a chance to display the family wealth, and that made soap a must-have. A bar of soap, cut from a larger cake, was heavily taxed and outside the reach of any but the rich, so of course they had to have it. The complexion could then be finished off with a quick splash wash of virgin milk, a popular facial tincture, and a spritz of scented water to ensure the requisite Regency glow.

# THE REGENCY SMILE

Of course, all the perfume and glow in the world wasn't worth a bean if your mouth was filled with blackened stumps or if your breath could knock out a suitor at a hundred paces. Just like surgery, dental work fell to untrained practitioners and was carried out without the benefit of anaesthetic. Marie Antoinette herself underwent agonizing cosmetic dental procedures prior to her wedding to Louis XVI, and though this was a good few decades earlier than the Regency, things had changed very little in the intervening years. As in all things, prevention was better than cure, and in the Regency oral hygiene was just part of the daily routine. With modern toothpastes not yet available, people used a toothbrush and tooth powder, which was purchased from apothecaries along with any other bits and bobs needed for home medicine and hygiene. Just like today, manufacturers made impressive claims about their products, promising that their tooth powder could work miracles.

> *[Mr Turner's tooth powder] is considered as pleasant*
> *in its application, as it is excellent in its effect;*
> *it renders the teeth smooth and white, braces the*
> *gums, makes them healthful, red and firm, prevents*
> *decay, toothache, that accumulation of tartar (so*

*destructive to the teeth and gums) and imparts*
*to the breath a most delectable sweetness.*[33]

Sometimes, one could even mix one's virtues and one's vices. Queen Charlotte was a snuff maniac and used a tooth powder made of snuff blended with red earth, which she moistened with green tea before use. Some fine tooth powders were made from ground-up coconut shells, while others contained charcoal or even the ground crusts of bread that had been deliberately burned black. With charcoal hopefully freshening the breath, abrasives such as salt, eggshells and even ground-up china were added to a mixture of cream of tartar, borax and a host of other ingredients. This resulted in a product that might scrape away at the enamel and which tasted a fright, so manufacturers threw in honey or fragrant oils, such as peppermint or orange, to make users a little less likely to gag during their brushing.

If, despite your very best efforts, you lost some teeth, the only option was to turn to dentures. Should money be no object then so-called mineral teeth, made from porcelain, would fill the gap. Alternatively, you could splash out on a set of Waterloo teeth, harvested from soldiers killed at the Battle of Waterloo. These were boiled and set into ivory dentures and were definitely not for the faint-hearted!

# FEMALE TROUBLE

There were, of course, concerns particular to women that would've given any gal pause for thought as she gadded about in her delicate white gown, fostering a rosy glow and learning how to finger her harp. Being delicate, accomplished and eminently eligible was one thing, but as a girl matured and went through puberty she would have had her period to deal with on top of everything else. So how did our Regency females deal with a situation that was, by definition, going to come up time and time again?

*The greatest care is then necessary, as the future health and happiness of the female depends in a great measure upon her conduct [during her period].*

*She should be careful to take exercise daily in the open air, to partake of a wholesome nutritious diet, and not to indulge in tight clothes ... one seldom meets, at this period, with complaints from obstruction among the more active and industrious part of the sex; whereas the indolent, inactive, and luxurious, are seldom free from them.*[34]

For women of the era, dealing with periods was a necessary chore, and for those of the ton it was arguably a little easier than for those who had jobs that required them to labour for hours every day. Historian Lucy Inglis uncovered the truth about sanitary care in the Georgian era, and it may surprise you to learn that women used something akin to the modern tampon, known as *suppositories*. These were sticks a few inches in length which were wrapped in linen and stitched together around a dangling cord. They were used just like today, then washed and used again. Alternatively, little bags filled with padding were inserted into the vagina until the wadding was saturated, at which point it was replaced and the bag reinserted. For women who preferred to use a towel or needed extra protection to deal with a heavy flow, a belt was worn which was attached to a piece of padded muslin, essentially making an early sanitary pad. They were boiled and used again as required.

Though we may not give much thought to such things when watching *Bridgerton* or leafing through the pages of a favourite Jane Austen novel, facts of life such as these have always been dealt with by the women who had to live with them. It's not surprising that precious little information about this has survived from an era when expectations of women and so-called ladylike behaviour were so stringent.

# PREGNANCY

Though upper-class marriages could be made for anything from love to business, the aim was always dynastic. It was the duty of the newly married couple to produce children as soon as possible, to ensure the succession of their money, estates and titles. As Bridgertonians know, the Duke of Hastings was determined not to father any children at all. When Daphne became his bride, she believed that he was unable to be a father, not that he had made a conscious decision to remain childless. She felt deceived and, in a controversial episode, refused to let Simon withdraw during sex. Though Daphne didn't conceive at that point, it seemed as though the couple's marriage wouldn't survive. As viewers know, that wasn't quite how things turned out.

For those women who fell pregnant outside of marriage, things were very different. For the ton, to be pregnant and not married was the height of shame. It was one thing to be left like Violet Bridgerton, widowed by a bee sting while with child, but to be an unmarried single mother was beyond the pale. This will be familiar to *Bridgerton* fans, who saw Marina arrive from her rural home to stay with the Featheringtons, that family little realizing what was ahead. Although Marina's appearance at the Danbury Ball made a splash with potential suitors and landed her the coveted title of Lady Whistledown's diamond – 'the incomparable' – she soon took to her bed with a mysterious illness. Eagle-eyed viewers will already have spotted a clue that Marina was not as carefree as she seemed, thanks to the lover's eye necklace she wore. A lover's eye was a small painted miniature of the eye of one's beloved, and the fact Marina sported one suggested her heart belonged to another. To add more drama, it soon became apparent that Marina wasn't unwell – but pregnant.

Thinking herself abandoned by her unborn child's father, soldier Sir George Crane, Marina accepted the proposal of the unsuspecting Colin, with an aim of marrying as quickly as possible. However, she lost both her reputation and her fiancé when society learned that she was with child. With the Featheringtons unable to buy her a place in hospital, a desperate Marina attempted to abort her baby by brewing a tea of juniper that she hoped would induce a miscarriage. It was an act that was all too common in the Regency, when desperate women resorted to herbal teas made with the likes of juniper or pennyroyal in the hope that they would end an unwanted pregnancy. In the event, Marina's efforts were unsuccessful and she learned that George had actually been killed in action. Though many women would have faced an uncertain and humiliated future, Marina was offered a bittersweet solution. When the brother of her unborn child's late father offered to marry her to fulfil George's obligation, Marina accepted. In doing so, she settled for a marriage that might not have been a love match but which offered her security and at least contentment.

To be the mother of an illegitimate child was to face a future of shame, gossip and certain shunning by polite society. For the father of such a child, the consequences were less severe. Though his actions would be frowned upon, he would be neither shunned nor disgraced. He would still be considered an eligible bachelor and would be welcome in society just as he was before he became a father.

For those couples of the ton who were struggling to conceive, there was little practical help available from the respected and expensive accoucheurs (male midwives) to whom they turned for advice. These learned men of medicine would generally fall back on the standard advice offered to women in the Regency and encourage them to take the waters or go somewhere that offered clean, fresh air. If that failed, they resorted to bloodletting, which would have no impact whatsoever on a woman's fertility. You will note that when it came to matters of fertility, the focus fell on the hopeful mother rather than her husband.

Once a woman of the upper class fell pregnant, everything revolved around the delivery of a healthy baby. Above all, doctors believed that ensuring the stability of her constitution in the early stages of the pregnancy was vital for hopefully ensuring a relatively easy time in childbirth. Likewise, light exercise was encouraged during early pregnancy; essentially, avoiding any form of agitation was at the heart of the philosophy. While women continued with their social engagements, as the pregnancy progressed and her lying-in period approached, the mother-to-be was gradually weaned off her commitments in preparation to take to her bed.

As the due date approached, a woman's diet was strictly monitored, and if her bump began to get too big she would be induced to vomit in order to keep her baby at a deliverable size. Alternatively, she might be starved in order to achieve the same end – and we are well aware now that neither of these are ideal treatments for pregnant women. Likewise, medical manuals of the era reveal that bleeding was a popular cure for just about any ailment an expectant mother might encounter. Although some physicians allowed very light exercise late in the pregnancy, it was most common for an expectant mother to endure a lying-in period in which she was put to bed and forbidden from taking any exercise at all for anything between several weeks and several months.

During lying-in, the lady simply waited for her labour to begin, counting down the days until her contractions started. As soon as she went into labour, all the windows and doors of the lying-in room were closed, and the room itself was warmed to ward off any drafts that could cause either the mother or her newborn to catch the dreaded fever. In this virtual hothouse the very bacteria that the medics hoped to keep away were free to thrive, and with no fresh air to speak of it must have made an already difficult experience all the tougher. Yet though pregnancy carried risks, the mother-to-be had yet to endure the most dangerous time of all: giving birth.

# CHILDBIRTH

Another concern that was limited to women was, of course, childbirth. Though Queen Charlotte had given birth to fifteen children, all but two of whom lived to adulthood, the risks associated with delivering a baby in the Regency were considerable even for the elite, despite their ability to afford the very best physicians money could buy. In fact, when the Queen herself gave birth, her own very expensive physician had stood back to allow Mrs Draper, an elderly midwife, to do what she did best and deliver the heir and spares.

The chance of dying in childbirth or soon after was considerable, with a fifth of mothers not surviving. However, in a world where it was expected that the women of the ton would get on with securing the line of their husband's succession, it was something that simply couldn't be avoided. In his desperation *not* to become a father, *Bridgerton*'s Duke of Hastings was refusing to fulfil the most important dynastic duty of all. He may have had his reasons, but we need only consider the scramble of the Regent's brothers to marry and produce heirs once Princess Charlotte of Wales died to see just how unlikely a scenario it was.

When it came to childbirth, there were few options available beyond the traditional pushing, aided by the physician or midwife, and labour could be an agonizing and incredibly dangerous experience for mother and baby alike. Few pregnancies used forceps, and the risk of infection meant Caesarean sections were more often than not reserved for the delivery of babies whose mothers had passed away during labour. The threat of infection was enormous, and even after childbirth a new mother wasn't out of the woods. She would remain in her stifling sealed room and be kept on a mostly liquid diet, denied access to the very nourishment that would help her recover. 'The woman should avoid company and noise' was the advice. 'With regard to her diet, it should, for the first week at least, be very light, and of easy digestion.'[35]

*Nothing is more certain than that the mismanagement of pregnancy lays the foundation of many diseases, which occur after delivery, and for which the medical attendant is blamed, when the cause was wholly attributable to the misconduct of pregnancy, either from false ideas of the woman herself, or the absurd advice of her friends.[36]*

The sad fate of the Prince Regent's only legitimate child was proof, if any were needed, of the danger of being a woman in the early 1800s. Princess Charlotte was just twenty-one when she died in childbirth, her still-born son and the physician completing the 'triple obstetrical tragedy'.

Pregnancy, labour and the immediate period after childbirth were enormously hazardous times for a mother, but with the belief that too much emotion was in itself dangerous, the decisions on her care were frequently taken out of her hands altogether. One might think that, with money to pay for the very best healthcare, upper-class mothers were at less risk of complications than those in the working classes. As the tragic case of Princess Charlotte of Wales shows, however, that was not necessarily the case.

Princess Charlotte was the only child of the Prince Regent and his hated wife, Caroline of Brunswick. She was the heir to the throne, and with none of the prince's siblings having produced legitimate children of their own she was also the best hope for the line of succession. Princess Charlotte married her husband, Prince Leopold of Saxe-Coburg-Saalfeld, in 1816 and fell pregnant soon after. Her care was entrusted to Sir Richard Croft, an eminent accoucheur who had tended many noble families and served as a physician to George III.

In keeping with his usual methods and those common for the time, Croft kept his patient on a restricted diet almost to the point of starvation and further weakened her with bloodletting as the months went on. Charlotte was expected to deliver her child on 19 October 1817, but the date came and went and still she remained lying-in with no sign of labour. Croft permitted her to take gentle walks in the hope that the activity might encourage the baby to appear, and she even drove out in a carriage with her husband until, on 3 November, her first contractions began.

Charlotte laboured on for two days, growing weaker and more desperate with every passing hour. Sir Richard refused her any food, and he and his colleagues continued to wait as the princess continued to suffer. It may be that the use of forceps could have made all the difference, but they were rarely used except in cases where a mother had died during labour. Sir Richard never used them and was not about to make an exception in this important case.

Princess Charlotte finally gave birth to a stillborn baby boy on the evening of 5 November 1817. The child was large, weighing 9 pounds, but every effort to resuscitate him was unsuccessful and the exhausted new mother learned that her suffering had been in vain. She answered simply, 'It is the will of God,' then sank back to rest. A few hours later, Princess Charlotte began to suffer violent abdominal pains and started vomiting uncontrollably. Sir Richard Croft returned to her bedside to find the princess bleeding, gasping for breath and freezing cold to the touch. Sadly, his efforts to save her came too late: just hours after the delivery of her stillborn child, Princess Charlotte of Wales died.

*The most melancholy and distressing event has happened – Princess Charlotte is no more! All is dismay and grief, rejoicing turned into mourning, in the death of the most lovely and affectionate of princesses. The scene at this time exceeds all attempt at description.*[37]

The death of the beloved princess shook the nation. People all over Great Britain went into mourning in scenes that were, at the time, unprecedented. In their grief the people looked for someone to blame, and they turned on Sir Richard Croft, who could not forgive himself for the death of Charlotte and her baby. Just three months later he shot himself, putting the final act to what came to be known as the 'triple obstetrical tragedy'.

# CHAPTER SEVEN

# LOVE AND MARRIAGE

'Remember that it is the affections of a sensible
and reasonable soul you hope to subdue, and
seek for arms likely to carry the fortress. He that
is worthy, must love answering excellence.'

*The Mirror of the Graces*[38]

**R**omance is central to the world of *Bridgerton*, and central to the world of Regency upper-class romance was the marriage mart. Viewers of the first season watched Daphne try to navigate the sometimes choppy waters of society as a young debutante coming out for her first Season and facing all the trials and temptations that the world could throw at her. The road to a happy ending was paved with passion and intrigue, and audiences couldn't get enough.

Young women of the ton came out when they reached their late teens, at which point they would dress in their finest white gowns and gloves, put on just enough make-up to make it appear that they were entirely fresh-faced and step out at Queen Charlotte's Ball. There, they would be observed by the Regency's most eligible bachelors and their families, who scrutinized each girl just as each girl's parents scrutinized their opposite numbers. This, after all, was where marriages could be made.

# QUEEN CHARLOTTE'S BALL

Queen Charlotte's Ball began in 1780, as a way for the philanthropic Queen to raise funds for her favourite charities. She stood beside a monumental birthday cake and greeted each debutante as they were presented to her by their high-ranking sponsors, just as Lady Danbury sponsored the Sharmas, marking their coming out into society as marriageable women. Queen Charlotte used the money raised to fund Queen Charlotte's and Chelsea Hospital, and the ball became an annual event, continuing long after her death. Charlotte herself wasn't overly fond of the occasion, though, as was noted by waspish diarist Horace Walpole: 'The crowd at the birthday was excessive, and had squeezed, and shoved, and pressed upon the Queen in the most hoyden manner. As she went out of the drawing room, somebody said in flattery, "The crowd was very great." – "Yes," said the Queen, "and wherever one went, the Queen was in everybody's way."[39]

Coming out cost money, from gowns to dowries to tickets to balls and other necessities, but it had to happen if a daughter of the ton was to marry. Once a girl had come out, she was part of the marriage mart, chaperoned from ball to rout to any other social event where eligible young men might be present. Here, those hard-won dancing skills really came into their own as she tried to catch the eye of her and her family's preferred candidate, while hopefully avoiding those she'd rather not get to know.

Each young lady brought with her a dowry, namely an amount of money and perhaps land or other valuable chattels that would become the property of her husband upon marriage. A fat dowry could make a girl very desirable indeed, while, as the Featherington daughters discovered, no dowry meant no real prospects for a happy ending, barring a miracle. In the Regency, young men and women were not so different from today, and they knew who they were attracted to and who they weren't. Unlike today, though, they couldn't simply strike up a conversation and get to know somebody just because they wanted to.

# GETTING TO KNOW YOU

The reputation of a young woman had to be protected at all costs, and this meant that if an introduction was to be made, it had to be done formally. Acquaintances could be made by family members or respectable intermediaries at parties or other events, and at a dance a formal meeting had to have taken place before a lady could agree to partner a gentleman. To do otherwise would be the height of impropriety. And to make matters worse, one could not be presented to a person of a higher social rank unless the latter was happy to receive the introduction. These rules were strict and unbending, and in a time when reputation was everything few were willing to risk damaging it.

> *Females, whose sphere is more confined than that of men, find at once in the practice of this art, exercise and an opportunity of displaying their native graces. Where only gentle exercise is desirable, the minuet offers its services with the greatest effect; and when elegantly danced, affords the greatest pleasure to the spectators.*[40]

Dances gave a rare chance for private conversation and the touching of hands away from chaperones, but other than that any form of physical contact was almost unthinkable. When

Daphne and the Duke of Hastings stole a kiss in the garden and were discovered by Anthony, the consequences could have been far-reaching for Daphne. Anthony was scandalized and insisted that Simon marry Daphne, but the duke refused and preferred to fight a duel rather than marry. Yet for Daphne, had word of the kiss got around, the future would have been bleak. No family would have wanted her to marry their son and no man would have considered her a suitable bride. A man might help a lady into a carriage should she need it, but even then discretion had to be applied. After all, one wrong move and a woman's reputation could be ruined – though that of the man would survive intact. It's unfair and hypocritical, but it was simply a fact of Regency life.

Once a couple had decided that they wanted to be together, they would present themselves as a pair. This meant taking chaperoned walks in front of their peers, dancing together and generally appearing as a twosome. It also gave families an opportunity to show off their new connection, just as the Sharmas and the Bridgertons did when they promenaded together after the engagement of Edwina and Anthony. It didn't mean canoodling or PDAs, of course, and everything stayed truly respectable. It wasn't enough simply to *be* respectable; one had to make it clear to everyone that was the case. When Eloise visited Theo alone without a chaperone, she little expected Lady Whistledown to reveal the burgeoning relationship to all of society. Though Lady Whistledown's motives might have been pure, the impact on Eloise and her family was disastrous. Faced with the dual scandal of their daughter fraternizing alone with a man, and a radical at that, the Bridgertons found themselves at the centre of society gossip all over again. For a lady to be unchaperoned in the company of a man was so unthinkable that Queen Charlotte wouldn't even let her adult daughters be alone with their uncles, insisting there always be a chaperone present. Being pure wasn't enough if one wasn't seen to be pure too.

A couple take a walk together, declaring themselves to society as a connected pair.

Unless a couple planned on eloping, which no truly respectable couple would have dared do, once a suitable match had been found and both sets of parents were agreeable, a proposal could be made. Of course, a woman would never propose to a man but must instead wait for him to make the move. Long engagements weren't common, and neither were long courtships. If a lady found a match in her first Season, she should expect to be firmly married off by the start of the next. Her days of girlhood were over, and she could only hope that she had made a good choice.

*He that is worthy must love answering excellence.*
*Which of you all would wish to marry a man merely*
*for the colour of his eye, or the shape of his leg?*
*Think not, then, worse of him than you would do of*
*yourselves; and, hope not to satisfy his better wishes*
*with the possession of a merely handsome wife.*[41]

For those who found no match, there was always a second Season and perhaps even a third, but with each year that passed her prospects grew dimmer. We have already considered the plight of the spinster, reliant on her family for support, and the thought of that was abhorrent to the debutantes of the ton. Marriage was the next step on what was essentially a career ladder for which they had been trained since early childhood. There were precious few alternatives. Yet while ladies were being prepared for marriage, gentlemen could be focused on rather less domestic pursuits.

# DUELS OF HONOUR

After Anthony stumbled across his sister and the Duke of Hastings in a heated clinch, the two men engaged in a duel to defend Daphne's honour. Though unthinkable to us today, duelling was a familiar, if mostly illegal, practice throughout Europe and offered two combatants the chance to settle a disagreement with honour, albeit with occasionally fatal results. If a gentleman took offence at another's behaviour, he could issue a challenge and demand satisfaction; in short, he challenged him to a duel.

Once this was done, it was considered dishonourable to reject the contest. The only exception came if a gentleman considered his opponent of a lesser rank, such as a criminal or servant. In these circumstances alone could he reject the challenge without a stain on his honour. Otherwise, the clash had to be accepted and the duel proceeded, subject to very strict rules of etiquette.

Each gentleman chose a trusted second, whose first job was to meet and attempt to resolve the issue without recourse to weaponry. If the offending gent was willing to apologize and the upset party could accept without sacrificing his honour, this was a chance to forestall the encounter. This could not happen if physical blows had been exchanged, in which case the challenger was also given the opportunity to whip his opponent, in addition to an apology.

Where an apology was not offered or was given but rejected, the duel went ahead. Generally, the chosen weapon was pistols, though some preferred swords. In the event, the aim usually wasn't to kill an opponent but merely to satisfy wounded honour. Either the shots were fired at the same time or the offended party was given the first shot and his opponent would hope it would be fired deliberately over his head. Then, the gentleman who had caused the initial offence could choose to shoot at his adversary, to fire into the air or not to fire at all. After each round the seconds would ask whether the insulted man had received satisfaction. Once the challenger agreed that he had, the duel was ended.

Because such battles of honour were illegal and usually symbolic rather than intended to cause bloodshed, they tended to take place early in the morning in a secluded spot. If a duel resulted in death, the gentleman who had fired the offending pistol or wielded the offending sword would face the courts and a potential death sentence. In reality, most duels were resolved without any fatalities and often only wounded pride.

# MARRIAGE

Hopefully, any duels would be dispensed with swiftly, if they were to happen at all, so the would-be groom could get back to the business of his marriage. Once a proposal had been accepted, there were several options open to the happy couple. Most common was to have the wedding banns read in church for three Sundays prior to the date of the wedding. Alternatively, if time was of the essence, a common licence could be obtained from a bishop to expedite the process. The third option was to get a prohibitively expensive special licence, which could only be obtained from the Archbishop of Canterbury. This licence allowed a couple to be married at any time and in any location. It was this type of licence that Simon and Daphne obtained in *Bridgerton*, but they went one step better and received their licence from the Queen herself. That's life in the elite social strata for you.

Just like today, a wedding could be as humble or as lavish as expenses allowed, but it was another chance to show off just how much money a family possessed. Unlike modern weddings, the ceremony itself was a very intimate affair, limited to the bride and groom, their witnesses, bridesmaids, groomsmen and close friends and family. Of course, the weddings of the elite would see everyone in their newest finery, with the wedding gown the height of fashion, though white bridal dresses were not yet the norm. Having said that, in a world where fashionable ladies favoured white anyway, it was by default a popular choice. Families could really push the boat out with the celebrations that followed, launching the newly-weds into what would hopefully be a long and happy marriage.

And if you were one of the newly-weds, you really did hope things would work out, because in the Regency *till death do us part* wasn't just an expression. As the Prince Regent himself had learned when he separated from his wife within eighteen months of their marriage, obtaining a divorce in Regency England was no easy matter. He never achieved it, and for those who did the stakes could be high and the cost ruinous in every sense.

# UNHAPPILY EVER AFTER

Until the passing of the Matrimonial Causes Act of 1857, which legalized divorce in the civil courts, it was governed by the ecclesiastical courts, and the Church didn't end a marriage without very, very good reason. Even these divorces didn't allow a couple to remarry, though, and they were more akin to what we would today call a legal separation, with no shared legal or financial responsibilities going forward. It was freedom, but only to a point.

The only way to obtain a complete dissolution that allowed for remarriage was to secure a parliamentary divorce, and these were notoriously difficult to obtain. They began with a criminal conversation case, because they relied on adultery by one of the parties to make them even a slight possibility. If a woman committed crim. con., her life in polite society was over. Though she wasn't the one being charged, as her husband would actually sue her alleged lover, it was the woman who would be ruined in the eyes of society and ostracized from all that she had known. Worse still, her money and property remained in the hands of her husband, as did her children.

For men, of course, things were different. As his former wife counted the cost of her ruin, a divorced husband might even drink at a club with the third party who had effectively broken up his marriage. Even the law itself was unequal: a man could divorce his wife through Parliament for adultery, but she could not do the same to him. If a woman wanted to bring a case of crim. con. for adultery, it had to be aggravated with either physical abuse, bigamy or incest, and all of these were notoriously difficult to prove. The law, like so many other things, was far from fair.

Once the suit for criminal conversation had been concluded in favour of the supposedly innocent party, the marriage was still not over. The second stage, an expensive parliamentary divorce, was the final process that would end the union.

Many simply chose to remain separated and not remarry, hoping to avoid a media frenzy. Rather than see their names and most intimate business splashed across the newspapers, they contented themselves with mere separation.

If the divorce went ahead, however, a Private Act of Divorcement was brought before Parliament, then read three times before the Lords. Witnesses were brought to testify against the adulterous party, but the defendants, often the wives of powerful and rich men, could not testify on their own behalf, meaning their voices were not heard before the Lords made their decision. It's unlikely they would have swayed the verdict one way or another even if they were.

If a divorce was granted, the loss to the adulterous party – if it was the wife – was huge. She surrendered everything in return for an allowance that was far from generous and which frequently went unpaid. Denied access to what had once been her assets, few could afford to countersue. She might be free, but she was, in the social and often financial sense, ruined.

# SPINSTERS AND WIDOWS

Although every family hoped that their daughters would make a good marriage, not all women became wives, whether by accident or design. However, those who remained spinsters faced challenges of their own. In the Regency spinsterhood was considered unnatural, and unmarried women were seen as figures to be pitied or even gossiped about as their peers wondered what might be wrong with them that had led them to fail in their expected duty.

As discussed elsewhere, many spinsters were beholden to their families to keep them. These families often regarded the women as financial burdens who should be reliant on a husband to keep them. For those unmarried women who had their own means, however, there was an opportunity for some level of independence, so long as their money hadn't been entrusted to male relatives to manage, which was frequently the case. It wasn't even a matter of simply finding a job to earn a living either, as career prospects for upper-class women were extremely limited. While becoming a governess or a companion to a lady offered a living, it was still seen as an undesirable position for a woman to be placed in and would have been a very significant step down in the ton.

For widows, meanwhile, there were also challenges ahead. When Edmund Bridgerton was killed by an allergic reaction to a bee sting, he left his pregnant wife and seven children to fend for themselves. Even as Violet mourned the husband she adored, she was faced with an uncertain future and a world she would have to navigate alone.

Regency widows were entitled to a jointure, or a third of the value of their deceased husband's estate, for the remainder of their lives, and that alone could be the difference between comfort and poverty. If a husband had been wealthy and his estates generated an income, his widow might find that her future was secure and stable, but if he was a gambler or spendthrift, things could be dark indeed. For those who found themselves in penury, a second marriage – if a husband could be found – might be their only route out of disaster. For a lady who achieved financial independence, however, marrying again might be the last thing on her mind.

Lady Featherington, of course, was anything but financially independent following her husband's death. Archibald's profligate and dissolute lifestyle meant that his wife and family were left in dire straits, and with no dowries to tempt husbands the marital prospects of his three daughters virtually disappeared. Because the Featherington estates were entailed on a male heir, meaning that only a male relation could inherit them, the women found themselves beholden to Jack, the new Lord Featherington. Although he was able to pay Philippa's dowry, he was determined to stamp his authority on his new estates and even moved Lady Featherington out of her bedchamber so he could occupy it. As he and Lady Featherington by turns battled and conspired over the marriages of her daughters and the family estates, the widow eventually began to realize where her true priorities lay.

The widows of peers were in a particular class of their own, as they retained their title until the heir to their late husband's title remarried. Then they would add 'dowager' to their title, to ensure no confusion between the current holder of the female title and the wife of the late peer. After the death of her husband and the succession of their eldest son, Anthony, Violet retained the title of Viscountess Bridgerton until Anthony married Kate. At that point, Kate became Viscountess Bridgerton and her mother-in-law adopted the modified title of Dowager Viscountess.

In some cases, the dowager would be expected to vacate the family home in favour of her replacement and move into her own dower house, though not every dowager followed this particular tradition. Even when they had such a house waiting, some widows preferred to hang around even after their son's new wife moved in, making their presence and wishes felt.

For those widows who did want to remarry, there were strict rules to follow. During the Regency era, custom dictated that a widow would not attend her husband's funeral. She was expected to go into mourning for twelve months, during which period no thought of remarrying should be entertained. After six months wearing black and a further six months transitioning from black into grey and other muted shades, she was allowed gradually to resume her social life. Only then could she think about marrying again, should she wish to do so.

# SEX

One thing *Bridgerton* isn't shy about is the sex lives of its heroes and heroines, and in a time when sex scandals reached as high as the heir to the throne himself, the bedrooms of the ton were busy places indeed. Yet as with so many things, there was a contradictory air to the relationship between society and sex. On the one hand, scandal and gossip were meat, drink and currency to the ton, but on the other they had to be seen to regard any immorality with as much distaste as they could muster.

When Daphne and the Duke settled down to enjoy their wedding night, Daphne was utterly innocent when it came to matters of sex. Today this seems highly unlikely, but in the Regency a young lady like Daphne could well have been utterly naïve on the subject of the birds and the bees. Though Daphne was able to take advice from a household servant, without an older sister, married friend or other acquaintance who was willing to clue them in, many young women would have been ill-prepared for their wedding night. It certainly wasn't part of the female education, and not every mother could be relied upon to have a frank talk with her daughter. In the case of the Queen, she simply tried to keep her daughters as girls, rejecting marriage proposals left, right and centre, but even in less extreme circumstances, sex education simply didn't exist for girls.

Young men in high society would have undertaken a Grand Tour while their female counterparts were preparing to come out. They would travel Europe and the Mediterranean, ostensibly on a cultural tour but one that allowed them to sample other delights too. Sex workers and brothels such as those patronized by Anthony were common in the Georgian and Regency eras, and these young men would certainly know a lot more than their female counterparts about the ways of the world. When the Regent married, he confided in a friend that he was horrified when his wife commented on the impressive size of his manhood; if she was pure and virginal, he argued, how would she have had another against which to compare it?

> *I have every reason to believe [that I was not Queen Caroline's first], for not only on the first night there was no appearance of blood, but her manners were not those of a novice. In taking those liberties natural on these occasions, she said, 'Ah mon dieu, qu'il est gros!', and how should she know this without a previous means of comparison?*[42]

The noblemen of the ton married for the purpose of continuing their dynasty, and once women were wives, work on the heir and spare began. For those who did want some form of birth control, perhaps to limit the rate at which pregnancies occurred, by far the most common method was that of withdrawal. Condoms weren't watertight and were of limited efficacy even in preventing sexually transmitted infections, but they were certainly useless when it came to contraception. In the long run, though, bearing children and continuing his dynasty was the very reason a nobleman married; he would not withdraw forever.

Common distinctions had it that men were sexual beings who had to release their libido, whereas passions of all kinds in women could only lead to trouble, from mental to physical to spiritual maladies, attributed on occasion to too much excitement. George III and Queen Charlotte had been bastions of morality, but the current incumbent, the weighty and debauched Prince Regent, could scarcely have set a more disparate example. He whooped his way across the south-east in a blaze of sexual glory – and in the case of his brothers, they went across the whole continent. They took mistresses, lived openly with women who weren't their wives and even conducted secret marriages that didn't stay secret for long. If they were expected to be the nation's moral compass, they failed at the first hurdle. It was little wonder the husbands of the upper class thought they could do as they wished.

Of course, affairs weren't limited to men. Jane Harley, the Countess of Oxford and Countess Mortimer, had so many children by so many different men that they were known as the Harleian Miscellany, but it was a rare husband who would put up with *that*. In the event, society didn't put up with it either, and Countess Mortimer found herself ostracized as a result of her choices. Women were subject to works such as Fordyce's joyless and restrictive *Sermons to Young Women*, which preached purity of spirit and mind as the only right path open to young ladies, with domestic and spiritual bliss a woman's reward should she comply. And in the ton, where life could be airless for young women, they had no choice but to toe the line. If discovered, a tryst such as that enjoyed by Kate and Anthony before her catastrophic accident would certainly ruin her opportunities for marriage and bring enormous shame to her family.

Men, on the other hand, were able to indulge their desires as freely as they wished, on the understanding that they caused their wives and families no embarrassment when doing so. Bridgertonians will recall Anthony's affair with opera singer Siena Rosso, a beautiful and mercurial woman who abandoned him to move up the social ladder. He receives a ticking off from his mother, but ultimately it was just one rite of passage in a young man's road to respectable adulthood. If one of his sisters had done similarly, her life as a lady would be over and her family would forever be singled out as one whose daughter had brought shame upon them.

When Lord Nelson openly cavorted with Lady Emma Hamilton, wife of his friend Sir William Hamilton, the celebrated naval hero *and* his mistress were spared from the disapproval of the people. Nelson was the national hero with the heart of oak, beyond reproach, and Lady Emma was a fashionista and social influencer par excellence. Instead, it was Nelson's cuckolded wife, Lady Frances, who was tutted about for refusing to tolerate her husband's fancy. Being well connected, fashionable and notorious could work wonders for a time, but when Nelson was dead and Lady Emma was in need, society rallied around the grieving and dignified Frances once more. Without the protection of her famed and worshipped lover, Lady Hamilton was just another 'other woman'.

The Ladies of Llangollen, Sarah Ponsonby (*left*) and Lady Eleanor Butler, were extraordinarily famous in their time, receiving visits from the likes of Lord Byron and William Wordsworth.

With all this focus on marriage and childbearing, you may be wondering where homosexuality and lesbianism found a place in Regency society. The answer is, unfortunately, not a happy one. Attitudes toward gay men were widely intolerant, and sodomy was punishable by death. The Bishop of Clogher, a man of enormous privilege, was forced to give up his identity and go on the run under an assumed name when he was discovered in a clinch with a guardsman. The bishop lived out his days as a butler in Scotland, while the guardsman took his bail and ran, never to be heard from again. This was a rare and extreme case, but to live openly as a gay man or woman was virtually unheard of. For those who dared to buck the trend, ostracism awaited.

Lesbians were barely even considered at all. Women such as the famed Ladies of Llangollen, who eloped together and lived as a couple for decades, were considered to be eccentric close friends and no more. There were few women like Anne Lister who dared to present themselves in masculine attire and take on the men at their own game, presiding as business leaders in their own right. When rumours spread that Anne had married another woman, anonymous adverts taunting the couple were placed in newspapers, but Gentleman Jack, as she was known after her death, lived unapologetically. Sadly, few women had the independent wealth to allow them to do so, and they were forced instead to conceal their desires just as their male counterparts did, for fear of being shunned or worse.

Once believed to be the richest commoner in England, Catherine Tylney-Long's was another tragic tale. Seduced for her wealth by a spendthrift rake who spent almost all of her enormous fortune, she was left to ruin, passing away estranged from her husband at just thirty-five.

Young ladies looking for love would do well to learn from the cautionary tale of Catherine Tylney-Long, the richest commoner in England. Catherine was young, intelligent and beautiful, and she had inherited a vast fortune in property and money that made her the subject of every fortune hunter in the land. After rejecting the suit of William, Duke of Clarence, also the future King William IV, she settled on marriage to dashing rake about town William Wellesley-Pole. Once the couple were married and all of Catherine's fortune bar a generous allowance fell into her husband's hands, things changed. He immediately changed his name to William Pole-Tylney-Long-Wellesley and got to work on spending the cash and sleeping with as many women as possible.

Through it all, Catherine stood by her man, even fleeing with him to Europe to escape his debts. He burned through his wife's fortune in a matter of years, and eventually her magnificent family home, Wanstead House, was sold to try to satisfy William's creditors. Only when he was sued by the husband of one of his conquests did Catherine make the break from William and return to England to try to rebuild her life.

William Pole-Tylney-Long-Wellesley barely tried to hide his reasons for marriage, taking his wife's illustrious names and rinsing her fortune to its last drop. Such was his villainy that he was denied custody of his children on Catherine's death, in a step wildly unusual for the Regency.

Catherine's abandonment sent William into a fury. He followed her to England and even attempted to abduct the couple's children. Laid low with illness, including the venereal diseases she had caught from her husband, Catherine tried to seek a divorce. Knowing that her health was in perilous decline, she made her children Wards of Chancery, meaning they could not be handed over to their father's custody in the event of her death. It proved to be a wise decision, for the woman who had once had it all died in 1825, aged just thirty-five. William suffered the indignity of becoming the first man ever to be denied custody of his own children because he was deemed morally unfit to care for them.

Yet though our hearts today must go out to Catherine, the press didn't see it quite that way. Instead, they turned the spotlight and blame back on her, suggesting this should be a cautionary tale to all young ladies who might seek an exciting spouse of their own. Let women put good sense first, they suggested, rather than their desires. It was a savage reading of a heartbreaking situation but one that tells us much about the morality of the day. Not every story could be Daphne and the Duke of Hastings, after all.

*Bridgerton* offers audiences a world of romance and passion, gossip and intrigue, but in the real world of the ton the life of a woman depended in great part on her reputation or even her perceived reputation. Though there were cautionary tales aplenty, there were also success stories, storybook romances and those who challenged the status quo at every turn. In reality as in fiction, some stories found their happy endings.

# AFTERWORD

**'*Fancy* and *Fashion* mingled
Sweet but to see, yet sweeter far to taste.'**

'Parties, Balls, Routs, &c., &c.', *The World of
Fashion and Continental Feuilletons*[43]

nd so we come to the end of our primer for life in the world of *Bridgerton*. If a Regency man had the good fortune to be born wealthy, he could look forward to a life of adventure, business and status. Many careers were open to him and, for the eldest son of an elite family, his path was already set. Of course, this might not be what a man wanted at all, but just as young ladies must follow the established rules of maidenhood and marriage, so too must their male counterparts follow their own rules of inheritance and respectability – within reason.

For young ladies, the world was one of deportment, propriety and being just intelligent enough to make a good society wife, without being so intelligent that it gave her ideas above her station. Toe the line, be modest and know how to manage a budget, and one day she too may become a Lady Patroness at Almack's. Aim high, as they say, and don't underestimate the importance of dancing.

# APPENDIX

Published in 1811, *The Mirror of the Graces* was a Regency lady's go-to manual for everything from dancing to cosmetics. The recipes below were included in the book for readers to make at home, whatever their cosmetic needs. They are reprinted here, with their original spellings intact, as a reference only; they have not been tested and their inclusion is not an endorsement.

# RECIPES

### Fard

This useful paste is good for taking off sunburnings, effects of weather on the face, and accidental cutaneous eruptions. It must be applied at going to bed. First wash the face with its usual ablution, and when dry, rub this fard all over it, and go to rest with it on the skin. This is excellent for almost constant use.

Take two ounces of oil of sweet almonds, ditto of spermaceti; melt them in a pipkin over a slow fire. When they are dissolved and mixed, take it off the fire, and stir into it one table-spoonful of fine honey. Continue stirring till it is cold, and then it is fit for use.

## Lavender Water

Take of rectified spirits of wine half a pint, essential oil of lavender two drachms, otto of roses five drops. Mix all together in a bottle, and cork it for use.

## Unction de Maintenon

*The use of this is to remove freckles. The mode of application is this: wash the face at night with elder-flower water, then anoint it with the unction. In the morning cleanse your skin from its oily adhesion, by washing it copiously in rose water.*

Take of Venice soap an ounce, dissolve it in half an ounce of lemon juice, to which add of oil of bitter almonds and deliquated oil of tartar, each a quarter of an ounce. Let the mixture be placed in the sun till it acquires the consistence of ointment. When in this state, add three drops of the oil of rhodium, and keep it for use.

## Crème de L'Enclos

*This is an excellent wash, to be used night and morning for the removal of tan.*

Take half a pint of milk, with the juice of a lemon, and a spoonful of white brandy, boil the whole, and skim it clear from all scum. When cool, it is ready for use.

## Pomade de Seville

*This simple application is much in request with the Spanish ladies, for taking off the effects of the sun, and to render the complexion brilliant.*

Take equal parts of lemon juice and white of eggs. Beat the whole together in a varnished earthen pipkin, and set on a slow fire. Stir the fluid with a wooden spoon till it has acquired the consistence of soft pomatum. Perfume it with some sweet essence, and before you apply it, carefully wash the face with rice water.

## Wash for the Hair

*This is a cleanser and brightener of the head and hair, and should be applied in the morning.*

Beat up the whites of six eggs into a froth, and with that anoint the head close to the roots of the hair. Leave it to dry on; then wash the head and hair thoroughly with a mixture of rum and rose water in equal quantities.

## Aura and Cephalus

*This curious recipe is of Grecian origin, as its name plainly indicates, and is said to have been very efficacious in preventing or even removing premature wrinkles from the face of the Athenian fair.*

Put some powder of the best myrrh upon an iron plate, sufficiently heated to melt the gum gently, and when it liquifies, hold your face over it, at a proper distance to receive the fumes without inconvenience; and that you may reap the whole benefit of the fumigation, cover your head with a napkin. It must be observed, however, that if the applicant feels any head-ach, she must desist, as the remedy will not suit her constitution, and ill consequences might possibly ensue.

## Eau de Veau

Boil a calf's foot in four quarts of river water till it is reduced to half the quantity. Add half a pound of rice, and boil it with crumb of white bread steeped in milk, a pound of fresh butter, and the whites of five fresh eggs; mix with them a small quantity of camphor and alum, and distil the whole. This recipe may be strongly recommended; it is most beneficial to the skin, which it lubricates and softens to a very comfortable degree. The best manner of distilling these ingredients is in the *balneum mariæ*; that is, in a bottle placed in boiling water.

## Virgin Milk

A publication of this kind would certainly be looked upon as an imperfect performance, if we omitted to say a few words upon this famous cosmetic. It consists of a tincture of benjoin, precipitated by water. The tincture of benjoin is obtained by taking a certain quantity of that gum, pouring spirits of wine upon it, and boiling it till it becomes a rich tincture. If you pour a few drops of this tincture into a glass of water, it will produce a mixture which will assume all the appearance of milk, and retain a very agreeable perfume. If the face is washed with this mixture it will, by calling the purple stream of the blood to the external fibres of the epidermis, produce on the cheeks a beautiful rosy colour; and if left on the face to dry, it will render it clear and brilliant. It also removes spots, freckles, pimples, erysipelatous eruptions &c., &c. if they have not been of long standing on the skin.

# IMAGE CREDITS

**Page 10:** New York Public Library / Look and Learn

**Page 13:** Wellcome Collection / Look and Learn

**Page 22:** *A Queen of Indiscretions*, Paolo Graziano Clerici, translated by Frederic Chapman, 1907

**Page 28:** Pierre de la Mésangère's *Journal des Dames et des Modes*, 1805 / Florilegius / Alamy

**Page 36:** Nicolaus Wilhelm von Heideloff's *Gallery of Fashion*, Vol. III / Metropolitan Museum of Art, New York

**Page 46:** *The Reminiscences and Recollections of Captain Gronow 1810– 1860*, John C. Nimmo, 1892 / British Library

**Page 53:** *Rijksmuseum*, Amsterdam / Look and Learn

**Page 57:** Rudolph Ackermann's *Repository of Arts, Literature, Fashions &c.*, July 1, 1823

**Page 62:** *La Belle Assemblée*, March 1808

**Page 68:** Portrait of Beau Brummell, Robert Dighton, 1805, Public Domain

**Page 74:** *Social England under The Regency*, Vol. II, John Ashton, 1890

**Page 88:** *The Follies & Fashions of Grandfathers*, Andrew W. Tuer, 1807

**Page 93:** *Le Chic á Cheval*, Louis Vallet, 1891

**Page 95:** *Old and New London*, Vol. IV, Edward Walford, 1878 / British History Online

**Page 98:** *Comforts of Bath*, Plate 8, by Thomas Rowlandson, 1798 / The Elisha Whittelsey Collection, The Elisha Whittelsey Fund, 1959, Metropolitan Museum of Art, New York

**Page 102:** *Clubs and Club Life in London*, John Timbs, 1872

**Page 104:** *The Beaux of The Regency*, Vol. I, Lewis Melville, 1908

**Page 106:** *The Pleasure Haunts of London*, E. Beresford Chancellor, 1925

**Page 108:** Arthur Wellesley, first Duke of Wellington, 1814, W. Say after T. Phillips / Wellcome Collection

**Page 113:** *Vaux-hall*, aquatint, Robert Pollard and Francis Jukes, after an engraving by Thomas Rowlandson / The Elisha Whittelsey Collection, The Elisha Whittelsey Fund, 1959, Metropolitan Museum of Art, New York

**Page 115:** *Carlton House*, North Front, c. 1819, aquatint, Richard Gilson Reeve after William Westall / Yale Center for British Art

**Page 125:** *The Trials of Five Queens*, R. Storry Deans, 1910

**Page 128:** 916 Collection / Alamy

**Page 133:** *Opening a Vein*, etching 1784–86 by Thomas Rowandson / The Elisha Whittelsey Collection, The Elisha Whittelsey Fund, 1959, Metropolitan Museum of Art, New York

**Page 147:** Princess Charlotte Augusta, stipple engraving by J. S. Agar after Charlotte Jones, 1814 / Wellcome Collection

**Page 156:** Pauquet's *Modes et Costumes Historiques*, 1864 / duncan1890 / Getty Images

**Page 171:** *The Ladies of Llangollen*, lithograph, J. H. Lynch after Mary Parker (later Lady Leighton), 1828 / Wellcome Collection

**Page 173:** The Picture Art Collection / Alamy

**Page 174:** History and Art Collection / Alamy

# BIBLIOGRAPHY

Aldrich, Robert and Garry Wotherspoon, *Who's Who in Gay & Lesbian History* (Abingdon-on-Thames: Taylor & Francis, 2020).

Anonymous, *The Ball, or A Glance at Almack's* (London: Henry Colburn, 1829).

Anonymous, *The Edinburgh Practice of Physic, Surgery, and Midwifery, Vol. 5: Midwifery* (London: G. Kearsley, 1803).

Anonymous, *George III: His Court and Family, Vol. 1* (London: Henry Colburn and Co., 1820).

Anonymous, *The Great Metropolis, Vol. 1* (Philadelphia: E. L. Carey and A. Hart, 1838).

Anonymous, *An Historical Account of the Life and Reign of King George the Fourth* (London: G. Smeeton, 1830).

Anonymous, *The Mirror of the Graces* (New York: I. Riley, 1813).

Anonymous, *The Quarterly Review, Vol. 270* (London: John Murray, 1938).

Baker, Kenneth, *George III: A Life in Caricature* (London: Thames & Hudson, 2007).

— —., *George IV: A Life in Caricature* (London: Thames & Hudson, 2005).

Barker, Hannah and Elaine Chalus (eds), *Gender in Eighteenth-Century England* (London: Routledge, 1997).

Barreto, Cristina and Martin Lancaster, *Napoleon and the Empire of Fashion* (Milan: Skira, 2011).

Black, Jeremy, *George III: America's Last King* (New Haven: Yale University Press, 2008).

le Bourhis, Katell (ed.), *The Age of Napoleon* (New York: Harry N. Abrams Inc., 1990).

Buchan, William, *Domestic Medicine, or A Treatise on the Prevention and Cure of Diseases by Regimen and Simple Medicines* (London: A. Strahan, 1790).

Campbell Orr, Clarissa (ed.), *Queenship in Europe 1660–1815: The Role of the Consort* (Cambridge: Cambridge University Press, 2004).

Clarke, John, *Practical Essays on the Management of Pregnancy and Labour* (London: J. Johnson, 1806).

Cole, Hubert, *Beau Brummell* (London: HarperCollins, 1977).

Colquhoun, Patrick, *A Treatise on the Wealth, Power, and Resources of the British Empire, in Every Country of the World* (London: Joseph Mawman, 1815).

Corfield, Penelope J., *The Georgians: The Deeds and Misdeeds of 18th-Century Britain* (New Haven: Yale University Press, 2022).

Craig, William Marshall, *Memoir of Her Majesty Sophia Charlotte of Mecklenburg-Strelitz, Queen of Great Britain* (Liverpool: Henry Fisher, 1818).

Cruickshank, Dan, *The Secret History of Georgian London* (London: Windmill Books, 2010).

Curzon, Catherine, *The Daughters of George III: Sisters & Princesses* (Barnsley: Pen & Sword, 2020).

— —., *The Elder Sons of George III: Kings, Princes & A Grand Old Duke* (Barnsley: Pen & Sword, 2020).

— —., *Kings of Georgian Britain* (Barnsley: Pen & Sword, 2017).

— —., *Queens of Georgian Britain* (Barnsley: Pen & Sword, 2017).

— —., *The Real Queen Charlotte* (Barnsley: Pen & Sword, 2022).

David, Saul, *Prince of Pleasure* (New York: Grove Press, 2000).

Dowden, Edward, *The Life of Percy Bysshe Shelley* (London: Kegan Paul, Trench & Co., 1887).

Dyer, Serena, *Material Lives: Women Makers and Consumer Culture in the 18th Century* (London: Bloomsbury, 2021).

Fitzgerald, Percy, *The Good Queen Charlotte* (London: Downey & Co., 1899).

— —., *The Life of George the Fourth* (London: Tinsley Brothers, 1881).

Fraser, Flora, *The Unruly Queen: The Life of Queen Caroline* (Edinburgh: A&C Black, 2012).

Graham, Thomas John, *Modern Domestic Medicine: A Popular Treatise* (London: privately published, 1827).

Greig, Hannah, *The Beau Monde* (Oxford: Oxford University Press, 2013).

Gronow, Rees Howell, *The Reminiscences and Recollections of Captain Gronow, Vol. 1* (London: John C. Nimmo, 1892).

Hadlow, Janice, *The Strangest Family: The Private Lives of George III, Queen Charlotte and the Hanoverians* (London: William Collins, 2014).

Hazlitt, William, *The Spirit of Controversy and Other Essays* (Oxford: Oxford University Press, 2021).

Heard, Kate, *High Spirits: The Comic Art of Thomas Rowlandson* (London: Royal Collection Trust, 2013).

Hedley, Olwen, *Queen Charlotte* (London: John Murray, 1975).

Hibbert, Christopher, *George III: A Personal History* (London: Viking, 1998).

— —., *George IV* (London: Penguin, 1998).

Hickman, Katie, *Courtesans: Money, Sex and Family in the Nineteenth Century* (London: HarperCollins, 2003).

Hicks, Carola, *Improper Pursuits* (New York: St Martin's Press, 2002).

Hilton, Boyd, *A Mad, Bad & Dangerous People?* (Oxford: Clarendon Press, 2006).

Inglis, Lucy, *Georgian London: Into the Streets* (London: Penguin, 2013).

Irvine, Valerie, *The King's Wife: George IV and Mrs Fitzherbert* (London: Hambledon, 2007).

Lacey, Brian, *Terrible Queer Creatures* (Dublin: Wordwell Ltd, 2019).

Law, Susan C., *Through the Keyhole* (Stroud: The History Press, 2015).

Lawrence, James, *The Empire of the Nairs, or The Rights of Women, Vol. 2* (London: T. Hookham Jr and E. T. Hookham, 1811).

de Plauzoles, Sicard, *Consumption: Its Nature, Causes, Prevention and Cure* (London: The Walter Scott Publishing Co. Ltd, 1903).

Roberts, Geraldine, *The Angel and the Cad* (London: Macmillan, 2015).

Robins, Jane, *The Trial of Queen Caroline: The Scandalous Affair that Nearly Ended a Monarchy* (New York: Free Press, 2006).

Smith, E. A., *George IV* (New Haven: Yale University Press, 1999).

Stott, Anne, *The Lost Queen* (Barnsley: Pen & Sword History, 2020).

Timbs, John, *Club Life of London, Vol. 1* (London: Richard Bentley, 1866).

Toynbee, Paget (ed.), *The Letters of Horace Walpole, Vol. 9* (Oxford: Clarendon Press, 1904).

Trusler, John, *A System of Etiquette* (Bath: W. Meyler, 1804).

Vickery, Amanda, *The Gentleman's Daughter* (New Haven: Yale University Press, 2003).

———., *Behind Closed Doors* (New Haven: Yale University Press, 2010).

Walker, Richard (ed.), *Regency Portraits* (London: National Portrait Gallery, 1985).

Wilson, Harriette, *The Memoirs of Harriette Wilson, Written by Herself*, *Vol. 1* (London: Eveleigh Nash, 1909).

———., *The Memoirs of Harriette Wilson, Written by Herself*, *Vol. 2* (London: Eveleigh Nash, 1909).


# NEWSPAPERS

All newspaper clippings are reproduced © The British Library Board; in addition to those cited, innumerable newspapers were consulted.


# WEBSITES CONSULTED

British History Online (http://www.british-history.ac.uk)

British Library Newspapers (https://www.gale.com/intl/primary-sources/british-library-newspapers)

Georgian Papers Online (https://gpp.royalcollection.org.uk)

Hansard (http://hansard.millbanksystems.com/index.html)

Historical Texts (http://historicaltexts.jisc.ac.uk)

House of Commons Parliamentary Papers (http://parlipapers.chadwyck.co.uk/marketing/index.jsp)

JSTOR (www.jstor.org)

The National Archives (http://www.nationalarchives.gov.uk)

Oxford Dictionary of National Biography (http://www.oxforddnb.com)

State Papers Online (https://www.gale.com/intl/primary-sources/state-papers-online-eighteenth-century)

The Times Archive (http://www.thetimes.co.uk/archive)

# ENDNOTES

## CLASS AND THE TON

1 Colquhoun, Patrick, *A Treatise on the Wealth, Power, and Resources of the British Empire, in Every Country of the World* (London: Joseph Mawman, 1815), p. 120

2 'Fashionable World', *Morning Post* (1818), issue 14958.

3 'Attack on the Prince Regent', *Leeds Mercury* (1817), issue 2693.

4 Anonymous, *The Quarterly Review, Vol. 270* (London: John Murray, 1938), p. 128.

5 Trusler, John, *A System of Etiquette* (Bath: W. Meyler, 1804), p. 4.

6 Ibid., p. 55.

7 Anonymous, *The Mirror of the Graces* (New York: I. Riley, 1813), p. 7.

8 Ibid., p. 164.

## FASHION

9 'A Poetic Epistle', *The Lady's Monthly Museum* (1802), vol. 8.

10 Anonymous, *The Dandy's Perambulations* (London: John Marshall, 1819).

11 'Newspaper Chat', *The Examiner* (1823), issue 816.

12 *The Mirror of the Graces*, op. cit., p. 31.

13 Ibid., p. 44.

14 Ibid., p. 43.

15 Ibid., p. 44.

## TRAVEL

16 Hazlitt, William, *The Spirit of Controversy and Other Essays* (Oxford: Oxford University Press, 2021), p. 328.

17 'The Parke', *Morning Post* (1810), issue 12277.

## SOCIAL OCCASIONS

18  'Parties, Balls, Routs, &c., &c.', *The World of Fashion and Continental Feuilletons* (1827), vol. 4, issue 39.

19  'The Political Examiner', *The Examiner* (1828), issue 1042.

20  Timbs, John, *Club Life of London, Vol. 1* (London: Richard Bentley, 1866), p. 287.

21  Anonymous, *The Great Metropolis, Vol. 1* (Philadelphia: E. L. Carey & A. Hart, 1838), p. 3.

22  'Vauxhall for One Shilling' (1833).

23  'Fashionable World', *Morning Post* (1811), issue 12602.

24  'Prince Regent's Fête', *Bury and Norwich Post* (1811), issue 1512.

25  'Carlton House', *The Times* (1811), issue 8325.

26  Dowden, Edward, *The Life of Percy Bysshe Shelley* (London: Kegan Paul, Trench & Co., 1887), p. 137.


## THE MEDIA

27  Lawrence, James, *The Empire of the Nairs, or The Rights of Women, Vol. 2* (London: T. Hookham Jr and E. T. Hookham, 1811), p. 160.

28  *The Examiner* (1812), p. 179.

29  'Mrs Clarke', *Morning Post* (1809), issue 11863.


## HEALTH AND HYGIENE

30  Buchan, William, *Domestic Medicine, or A Treatise on the Prevention and Cure of Diseases by Regimen and Simple Medicine* (London: A. Strahan, 1790), p. xviii.

31  Ibid., p. 449.

32  de Plauzoles, Sicard, *Consumption: Its Nature, Causes, Prevention and Cure* (London: Walter Scott Publishing Co. Ltd, 1903), p. 158.

33  Turner, W. S., *The Weekly Visitor, or Ladies' Miscellany* (1804), vol. 2, issue 73.

34  Graham, Thomas John, *Modern Domestic Medicine: A Popular Treatise* (London: privately published, 1827), pp. 460–61.

35   Anonymous, *The Edinburgh Practice of Physic, Surgery and Midwifery, Vol. 5: Midwifery* (London: G. Kearsley, 1803), p. 127.

36   Clarke, John, *Practical Essays on the Management of Pregnancy and Labour* (London: J. Johnson, 1806), pp. 1–2.

37   'Demise of Her Royal Highness the Princess Charlotte', *Morning Chronicle* (1817), issue 15138.

## LOVE AND MARRIAGE

38   *The Mirror of the Graces*, op. cit., pp. 214–15.

39   Toynbee, Paget (ed.), *The Letters of Horace Walpole, Vol. 9* (Oxford: Clarendon Press, 1904), p. 147.

40   Anonymous, *The Ball, or A Glance at Almack's* (London: Henry Colburn, 1829), pp. 77–8.

41   *The Mirror of the Graces*, op. cit., p. 205.

42   Robins, Jan, *The Trial of Queen Caroline: The Scandalous Affair that Nearly Ended a Monarchy* (New York: Free Press, 2006), p. 17.

## AFTERWORD

43   'Parties, Balls, Routs, &c., &c.', op. cit.

# INDEX